Testi...

# The More You Prospect, The More You Prosper

#1

Are you in a sales role where **YOU** need to make things happen?

If so this book is for you. Steve will guide you **step by step** to plan and execute at the highest level. He is uniquely positioned, based on **OVER 10,000 hours** to offer advice based on knowing what works but also knowing **what doesn't!** If you are coachable and looking to **go to the next level**, dig into this quick read and follow his advice....and get ready to make a **bigger impact** on the clients you serve.

David Patchen, Senior Vice President, Education and Practice Management, Raymond James Private Client Group

#2

This book is an absolute non-negotiable for every salesperson, manager, and leader. These 88 steps that Steve and Elaine have laid out is your compass and fundamental recipe to follow and coach, in order to optimize your sales output.

Kyle Fujimoto, Associate Athletic Director,
Ticket Sales & Service at University of Southern California

#3

The can-do attitude in this book is infectious and engaging and I truly believe the philosophy and mind set to be relevant to all aspects of business. I believe anyone in any role, especially sales, will benefit from reading this book and it should be a staple on every bookshelf regardless of the industry.

Sara Girton, Owner, Vision UTV

#4

This is the best book I have ever read on how to develop a prospecting mindset. It is relevant and practical and easy to implement. I only wish I had this book when I started my career in sales.

Ruben Flores,
Sales & Service Program and Execution Manager, AT&T

# THE MORE YOU PROSPECT,

# THE MORE YOU

# PRO$PER

**88 TIPS TO HELP
YOU IMPROVE YOUR
PROSPECTING
SALES SUCCESS**

**STEVE JOHNSON AND ELAINE JORDAN**

MINDSTIR MEDIA

Published by MindStir Media, LLC
45 Lafayette Rd | Suite 181| North Hampton, NH 03862 | USA
1.800.767.0531 | www.mindstirmedia.com

Printed in the United States of America.
ISBN-13: 978-1-962987-80-6

# CONTENTS

# INTRODUCTION

## My Background

I n 1985, I graduated from U. C. Irvine with a degree in psychology – I was in the half of the class that made the top half possible. Now, I know a lot of people say that, but in my case it was true. I had a 2.6 GPA with a BA in psychology. When it came to deciding on a career, I realized that I was not an accountant, attorney, engineer, or a doctor. Therefore, possibly like you, I decided to roll the dice and get into sales. After thirty-eight years in sales, I feel that I have earned a **PHD** – a degree in **P**ersistence, **H**ard work, and **D**etermination, and it has served me well.

I started to work for a very large international training company, Dale Carnegie, in downtown Los Angeles at the corner of Wilshire and Bixel on the seventeenth floor. I got $1,000 a month training salary for three months and then moved to straight commission. Many of you have probably read *How to Win Friends and Influence People* by Dale Carnegie or may have even taken a Dale Carnegie program. My job was to sell public speaking, sales, and leadership training programs to companies, so I was calling business to business in a zip-coded sales territory on the west end of the San Fernando Valley. My prospecting goals were 250 phone calls and ten face-to-face meetings per week.

My dad was my sales manager while I was at Dale Carnegie, and he told me he was going to help me to be a good salesman. He said, "I am not going to fish for you. I am going to teach you to fish." He got my business cards made for me, and I saw that my job title was salesman. I have never seen anyone in my life with the same title on their business card. I learned a lot in my first ten years in sales from him. He was more than my sales manager; he was also my hero. To me, he was the greatest salesman in the world. He was the typical American success story. He was the first-born son of two European immigrants and grew up on a dairy farm in Kansas City during the depression. He was honest and hard working. For the remainder of this book, I will just refer to him as my sales manager.

## DALE CARNEGIE TRAINING®

Offered by
Louis A. Johnson & Associates
1055 Wilshire Blvd., Suite 1703
Los Angeles, CA 90017-2449
Tel: 213.481.0800  Fax: 213.481.0988

**Steve Johnson
Salesman**

In my first ten years in sales, I made 120,000 calls and conducted 5,000 face-to-face meetings, failing 115,000 times. I failed 96% of every waking moment between the age of 22-32 to succeed only 4% of the time. I would make fifty outbound calls and set two meetings per day. I even told myself after I set those two meetings that even a broken clock was right twice a day. In that time frame, I became one of the top salespeople globally at Dale Carnegie Training and made the decision to go out on my own. Including my time at Dale Carnegie and the past twenty-eight years I spent running my own sales training company, I have been fortunate to work with some of the best sales organizations in the nation and have trained over 90,000 salespeople and 10,000 sales managers.

## Why I Wrote This Book

In the last thirty-eight years, I probably have made more mistakes and lost more sales than just about anybody I know. The opportunities lost from all the darn fool things I've done have been very costly. Fortunately, in this laboratory of human experience, this gauntlet I have run has enabled me over time to learn what works and what doesn't work. Also, I have been able to learn some of the best practices of some of the high-performing salespeople along the way. I have read many sales books that I knew were not written by anyone who has been in sales. They were written by those who did not walk, talk, or act like salespeople do, particularly when it comes to doing one of the most difficult elements of sales, which is prospecting.

I hope you will overlook and forgive me for using the personal pronoun "I." If there is anything in this book that sounds like I am bragging about myself, I did not intend it that way. Whatever self-promoting I've done was meant to highlight what these ideas have done for me and what they might do for anyone who applies them.

## Who This Book Is For

Who is this book for? If you believe that the largest room in the world is the room for improvement, then this book is for you. Specifically, it's for people who are thinking about a career in sales or are already in sales and are looking to improve their sales skills. It's for business owners, consultants, entrepreneurs, and anyone who has a product, service, or idea to sell. This book is ultimately for any salesperson who wants to get better.

Here is it. I hope you like it.

# PART I

# PROSPECTING MINDSET

**M**y sales manager told me, "The more you **learn**, the more you **earn**. If you read one book a month every month for the next five years, you will be an expert in what you do by the time you're twenty-seven years old."

Here are the first six books I read:

1. *How To Win Friends and Influence People.* By Dale Carnegie.

   o   Helped me with people skills, communication skills, listening skills.

2. *How To Stop Worrying and Start Living.* By Dale Carnegie.

   o   Helped me to live life one day at a time, how to solve problems and make decisions, and gave me productive ways to manage stress.

3. *The Quick and Easy Way to Effective Speaking.* By Dale Carnegie.

   o   Helped me to further develop my ability to speak in public, which increased my self-confidence.

4. *The Magic of Thinking Big.* By David Schwartz.

   o   Helped me to grasp the importance of goal setting in my life.

5. *How I Raised Myself from Failure to Success.* By Frank Bettger.

   o   Helped me with my selling skills.

6. *The Greatest Salesman in the World.* By Og Mandino.

   o   Helped me to understand the power of self-talk and positive affirmations and how you can use them to get and stay motivated to prospect. Had the biggest impact on my attitude and mindset.

In *The Greatest Salesman in the World,* there are ten affirmations. They were general affirmations that were designed to say repeatedly to yourself so they would sink into your subconscious mind…and they WORKED! The book got me to buy into the idea of the power of positive self-talk. While working at Dale Carnegie, I developed a number of affirmations that were very specific to situations I encountered as a salesperson where I needed to get and stay motivated.

In this chapter, I will walk you through the different positive affirmations and self-talk I have used over the past thirty-eight years to develop the right prospecting mindset. Not all will resonate with you, but I hope you find some that do.

If you would like to hear what these sound like, go to our YouTube channel and click on the Playlist **"Using Positive Self-Talk to Impact Your Prospecting Mindset."**

https://www.youtube.com/@NextLevelSalesConsulting/playlists

# TIP #1

# The more you prospect,
# the more you prosper!

One morning, my sales manager walked into my cubicle with a dictionary in his hand. I was wondering what he was up to. I thought he came by to have a conversation with me because I hadn't been putting up great sales numbers. He gave me the dictionary and asked me to look up the word prospect. I did.

"What does it mean?" he asked.

I said, "To look for gold."

He then asked me, "What word is beneath prospect?"

I said, "Prospector."

"What is a prospector?" he asked.

I said, "A person who looks for gold."

He asked, "What word is beneath prospector?"

I said, "Prosper."

He then asked me, "What is the definition of prosper?"

I said, "To be successful."

He said, "There it is on one page in the dictionary, all you need to know about what it takes to be successful."

I said, "What is that?"

He said, "The more you prospect, the more you prosper."

I began to think about how the more you prospect, the more you prosper and reflected on why I got into sales in the first place. It was so I could have uncapped income potential. I thought the harder I worked and the more skilled I became, the more money I could make and to put me in a better position to achieve some of my goals, like buying a new car and a house. I further realized that the key to achieving my goals was through prospecting and that the more I prospected, the more I would prosper. I began to say it to myself during the day to get and stay focused on prospecting, "Steve, the more you prospect, the more you prosper."

So, think about your goals right now. If you were to put in more time prospecting every day, do you think it would help you to move closer to achieving them? If so, try telling yourself that the more you prospect, the more you prosper. Making a few more prospecting attempts each day is a small feat to accomplish, but it counts a lot over an entire career.

**The more you prospect, the more you prosper.**

# TIP #2

# Get up now!

Our office was located at 1055 Wilshire Blvd., right down the street from the Los Angeles Chamber of Commerce. One day, a flyer from the chamber came to our office about Arnold Schwarzenegger coming to speak at the L.A. convention center at a fitness expo. I had read his book *The Education of a Body Builder* as a junior in high school when I was sixteen years old and playing basketball. I was 6'2" and weighed 150 pounds. I wanted to get stronger and decided to do so by lifting weights. I followed everything he said in the book in my workouts.

I decided to go to the event, and I'm glad I did. He was Mr. Olympia in 1980 and had just come out with the *Conan the Barbarian* in 1982, *The Terminator* in 1984, and *Commando* in 1985. He was still in incredible shape. The convention center was packed, and he told his story. Everybody in the audience was captivated by his accomplishments. When he was done, he said we had some time for questions.

The guy next to me raised his hand, and Arnold called on him. The guy asked, "Arnold, with all of these things you are doing, do you ever sleep?" Arnold basically said that sleep was a waste of time and that he only slept six hours per night. He went to bed at 10:00 PM and woke up at 4:00 AM. When his alarm went off, he said to himself, "Arnold, get up now." I thought that was awesome. Get up now. I was struggling with that, like many of us do. He then went on to say that, after he told himself to get up now, he would say to himself, "Arnold, you can lay in bed and dream, or you can get out of bed and **make your dreams come true**." He was so right. When the alarm goes off in the morning, the battle of mind over mattress takes place. That is when the self-talk begins.

I left that convention shot out of a cannon and went home to the apartment I was sharing with two of my friends. I wrote "Get up now" on a 3 X 5 card and tacked it to the ceiling of my room right above my bed. Almost every day since I saw Arnold give that speech, when my alarm goes off at 4:30

in the morning, I say to myself, "Steve, get up now. You can lay in bed and dream, or you can get out of bed and make your dreams come true."

So, tomorrow morning when your alarm goes off, tell yourself, "Get up now. You can lay in bed and dream, or you can get out of bed and make your dreams come true."

**Get up now.**

# TIP #3

# When you look good, you feel good, and when you feel good, you do good.

Working for Dale Carnegie, we were the guys in the white hats representing the company. Our calling card was *How to Win Friends and Influence People*. So how we dressed was important. My sales manager was very particular about dress, and his motto was "When you look good, you feel good, and when you feel good, you do good."

He had a simple dress code that I adhered to because of his beliefs about how prospects buy, which was that if a prospect wants to work with you, they will move heaven and earth to make that happen, and if they don't, any reason is as good as the next. You don't want that reason to be how you are dressed because that is one thing that is **under your control**. He said they will probably never tell you that, but you need to eliminate it as an objection before it comes up. So, he gave me a list of clothes to buy to build a wardrobe for my first year in sales. He instructed me to look at myself in the mirror every day after I got dressed for work and say to myself with enthusiasm, "When you look good, you feel good, and when you feel good, you do good."

Before I went into meetings, I would say to myself, "When you look good, you feel good, and when you feel good, you do good." I wanted to go into meetings with confidence and not be concerned about how I was dressed. We all know that you dress appropriately for your business environment, and if you aren't sure what's appropriate, you are better off going to a meeting a little overdressed than underdressed. It's hard to come back from that, especially if the meeting does not go well.

Many times, I have had prospects that became my clients tell me to ditch the suit and tie and come back for the next meeting in a pair of slacks and a navy blazer. Your body language is the most important thing you communicate. So, dress matters.

Tomorrow morning, when you are about to leave for work, look in the mirror and tell yourself, "When you look good, you feel good, and when you feel good, you do good." And before your first sales call of the day tell yourself:

**When you look good, you feel good, and
when you feel good, you do good.**

# TIP #4

# I feel good, I feel great, I've got sales to make, and I can't wait!

My first week on the job, I sat down with my sales manager, and he said, "Don't ever be late for work. We live in Los Angeles, and you know there will be traffic. So, try to give yourself a thirty-minute cushion for traffic, and if there isn't any and you get here a little early, so be it. Don't blame things on LA traffic, because you will be creating a bad habit immediately in your sales career of blaming. If you get here late, it is because you did not leave early enough. What time you decide to leave for work is under your control, so control when you leave in the morning."

He also said, "When you get here, be ready to start prospecting. Make a list of every prospect you want to call in the morning before you leave the day before so you can **walk right in and make things happen**."

He told me not to be like some of the other salespeople in the bullpen who come in late at 8:30 and blame it on traffic, talk to their co-workers until 9:00, build a plan for the day until 9:30, then take their first break and start prospecting at 10:00. Then they walk around the office with no energy or enthusiasm to prospect. He called them the sad singers and slow walkers, Sally Bad News and Johnny Hard Luck. Here they come, gloom and doom. Misery loves company.

He said, "You have to start talking to yourself in a positive way from the second you close the door of your car and keep talking to yourself all the way from the parking lot into the office. You need to walk a little quicker than you ordinarily do to get your body going and say to yourself every step of the way, **I feel good, I feel great, I've got sales to make, and I can't wait**. When you walk through the door of the office, go directly into your cubicle. Immediately begin your first call blitz of the day

11

by picking up the phone and calling the first number on the list you created the night before."

I loved it. I've said "I feel good, I feel great, I've got sales to make, and I can't wait" almost every morning for ten years as I walked into my office. When I got into the office, I couldn't wait to call prospects, get objections, go to voicemail, get my calls screened and, above all else, get meetings.

So, tomorrow morning when you get out of your car, or if you work at home as you walk into your office, say to yourself at least three times: "I feel good, I feel great, I've got sales to make, and I can't wait."

**I feel good, I feel great, I've got sales to make, and I can't wait!**

# TIP #5

# If it is to be, it is up to me!

There I was sitting in my office early in the morning one day, getting ready to begin my morning call blitz, when my sales manager came into my cubicle.

He looked at me and asked, "Do you know the ten two-letter words that will change your life?"

I said, "No, I don't. What are the ten two-letter words that will change my life?"

He said, "If it is to be, it is up to me, and those ten two-letter words are very important for you to say to your yourself every day before you start prospecting."

I said, "Why is that?"

He said, "Because prospecting is like shaving. Unless you do it every day, you are going to look like a bum. You need to have your bait in the water all the time." He went on to say, "No one is going to pick up the phone, knock on the door, go to the event, or ask for a referral for you. You are going to have to do all those things yourself. You need to get into the habit early on in your career of taking **personal responsibility** for your prospecting activity."

He said, "By telling yourself at the beginning of every day "If it is to be, it is up to me," you will, over time, develop that mindset. Repeating those words daily will set you up for success, not only now but in the future."

So I wrote "If it is to be, it is up to me" on a yellow sticky note and placed it right above my telephone. Every day when I got into the office in the morning, I reminded myself that prospecting is like shaving. Unless you do it every day, you are going to look like a bum. No one was going to do it for me.

So, I said to myself right before I began my morning call blitz, "If it is to be, it is up to me," then I made my first call — it was to my mom. I am the youngest of three and the last one to leave the house. She told me she was proud of me and that I was going to be a success and told me to have a good day. When the conversation was over, **I did not put the phone down**. I immediately got out my list of prospects that I planned to call that day and started calling. I kept on dialing until my morning call blitz was over. I utilized an underestimated element of making calls, which is **pace**. You slow down your pace when you put the phone down between calls. It is better to make one call right after another.

"If it is to be, it is up to me" became my battle cry in the morning. It sounded very Shakespearean to me. So I walked around my cubicle saying it like I was an actor on stage. I said it so many times to myself that I believed it — that **my destiny in sales was in my own hands.**

Take a yellow sticky note out right now and write: "If it is to be, it is up to me." Starting tomorrow, say it to yourself every day before you start prospecting. Those ten two-letter words could change your life.

**If it is to be, it is up to me!**

# TIP #6

# The time is now!

Here are some very common questions that I have asked myself a million times. What is the best time to call? Is there a time when prospects will be available and receptive to my calls? Is it better to call them in the morning than in the afternoon? Or are there some days of the week that are better than others?

I think the reason I was asking myself those questions was to see if there was some fantasy land where prospects always answered my calls, were in a great mood, and asked me to get together with them. As I tried to be honest with myself about why I was asking myself those questions, I realized that timing calls would not be a good habit to get into because self-talk like that wouldn't work. That was the advent of "the time is now."

- When I would say to myself, I can't call on Monday because people are getting ready for the week. I would tell myself, **the time is now** and make the call.
- When I would say to myself, I can't call in the morning because people are getting ready for the day. I would tell myself, **the time is now** and make the call.
- When I would say to myself, I can't call before lunch because people are getting ready to go to lunch. I would tell myself, **the time is now** and make the call.
- When I would say to myself, I can't call after lunch because people are just getting back from lunch. I would tell myself, **the time is now** and make the call.
- When I would say to myself, I can't call in the afternoon because people are probably in meetings. I would tell myself, **the time is now** and make the call.

- When I would say to myself, I can't call at the end of the day because people are getting ready to go home. I would tell myself, **the time is now** and make the call.
- When I would say to myself, I can't call on Friday because people are getting ready for the weekend and will probably be leaving early. I would tell myself, **the time is now** and make the call.

The time is now. **The time is always now**. With the time you spend being in your own head about if now is the right time to make a call, you could have already made the call and set a meeting. Don't overthink things — the time is now. Better to make the attempt and fail than to do nothing and flounder.

**The time is now.**

# TIP #7

# I'm doing them a favor!

The last four letters in the word enthusiasm are IASM – which stand for "I am sold myself." When you are sold on what you sell, it makes prospecting a lot easier. If you believe in yourself, your products, and your services, you will have the mindset that whenever you attempt to call a prospect you are doing them a favor, as opposed to being pushy, salesy, or an interruption in their day. It was a game changer for me to believe that, whenever I called a prospect, I was doing them a favor. It was almost like I owed it to them to try to meet them. Like I would be doing them a disservice by not calling them. Most salespeople never feel like that about what they do, but I did.

So how did I get sold on what I sold? I began to learn more about how our Dale Carnegie programs were helping our clients to overcome their fear of public speaking. In turn, they were able to do things they always wanted to do in their lives, like speak up in a meeting, attempt to get in a leadership role at their job, or sing in the church choir. Many times, when someone improves their public speaking skills, it gives them more confidence, which unlocks limitless possibilities for them in their lives. We were making a big difference in the lives of our clients, and it helped me to change my attitude about prospecting. I got rid of any of the sales self-consciousness that was holding me back. I had the attitude that, when I was making my fifty calls every day, I was doing those companies a favor by trying to meet with them to see if they had any employees who wanted to get better at public speaking.

I **had** to call them because I owed it to them. After all, we were starting a public speaking class at the Woodland Hills Marriott in six weeks. Not only did I feel like I was doing them a favor, but I also had a genuine sense of urgency to do so. As I reflected on my call reluctance, I realized the only problem I had was within the six inches between my own two ears.

That changed forever when I began to tell myself before I made a call that I was doing them a favor.

Every prospecting behavior you ever do will be a byproduct of your beliefs and values about prospecting. There are a lot of prospects out there that have a problem that needs to be solved. Before every prospecting attempt you make, remind yourself, "I'm doing them a favor."

**I'm doing them a favor.**

# TIP #8

# Don't think about what people think about you, because they don't think about you!

My first week in sales, my only job was to make one hundred calls per day so that I could get comfortable with picking up the telephone. I had a stack of old leads, and a script called the coffee talk. I was terrible. I was getting chewed up by gatekeepers, and when I would get a decision maker on the other end of the line, I didn't have a lot of confidence. When I got an objection, I felt that if I responded to it the prospect would think I was pushy or salesy.

I would then get up and walk around the bullpen and try to shake the rejection off. So, the number one salesperson on the team at the time came up to me and said, "I know what your problem is." I asked him what it was.

He said, "When you get rejected, you start walking around the bullpen like a prison warden. You have an over-inflated perception about what really happened. When you call and get rejected, the prospect hangs up the phone and goes on with their day. They don't sit there and analyze what you did by saying to themselves, 'Can you believe that Steve Johnson from Dale Carnegie just called? I can't believe he somehow muscled out one prospecting attempt today. His voice tone could have put a container of NoDoz to sleep. His value proposition was horrendous, and when I gave him an objection, he fell apart like a cheap suit. I am going to call his sales manager right now and give him feedback on Steve Johnson's call.' That never happens. They don't think a thing about you, and they go on with their day. Meanwhile, you're here wearing a hole in the carpet overthinking their reaction to your phone call."

He said, "Let me give you some advice. Don't think about what people think about you because they don't think about you. It is going to be impossible to be successful in sales if you're always concerned about what people are thinking about you, like being salesy, pushy, or an interruption in their day. If you are overly concerned about what others think about you, that's a tough cage to be in, being concerned about everyone's reaction to you. The healthiest thing you can say to yourself all day long if you have these concerns on your mind is to not think about what people think about you because they don't think about you."

I am so thankful I adopted this mindset. Don't think about what people think about you because they don't think about you. Learning this at twenty-two years old was very liberating.

So, if you ever find yourself overthinking making a call because you are worried that a prospect is going to think you are pushy, salesy, or an interruption in their day instead of not making the call, say to yourself, "Don't think about what people think about you, because they don't think about you." Then make the call.

**Don't think about what people think about you
because they don't think about you!**

# TIP #9

# Act enthusiastic and you will be enthusiastic.

In my first week in sales, I asked my sales manager, "What is one attribute I need to possess to be really successful in sales?" He told me that, if all I ever had was enthusiasm, that was all I would ever need. He was right. Here is how you maintain your enthusiasm. If you act enthusiastic, you will be enthusiastic.

Working in a bullpen, we were always doing things to get and keep each other motivated. One way we did this was to have competition with each other on who could make the most calls before lunch. The person who made the fewest number of calls had to buy the person who made the most calls whatever they wanted at El Pollo Loco down on Olympic and Union. They also had to leave the office to do so, which would cut down on their prospecting time. There was a triple whammy — you had the least number of calls, had to buy lunch, and had to leave the office to do so.

I am a competitive person and wanted to win that contest whenever we had one so I could get two free classic chicken burritos from El Pollo Loco. The downside of winning the burritos and eating them in the middle of the day is that they will be sitting in your gut when you still have the second half of the day to prospect, which can slow down your pace.

Our sales manager knew about our contest and what it could do to our prospecting productivity in the bullpen in the second half of the day, so he came back and showed us a way to keep our energy levels high. He told us that **motion creates emotion** and that if we acted enthusiastic, we would feel enthusiastic. He demonstrated how to enthusiastically say as a group that if you act enthusiastic, you will be enthusiastic.

Many of us are sitting down all day anyway, and "Act enthusiastic and you'll be enthusiastic" was a great way to get moving. Remember, if you

21

act enthusiastic, you will be enthusiastic, and that enthusiasm will come through in your voice on the other end of the line!

**Act enthusiastic and you will be enthusiastic.**

# TIP #10

# Hunker down.

I was getting worried because my commission checks were getting smaller, I was really struggling, and I realized that I was in my first sales slump. I went to my sales manager and asked him what I should do.

He said, "You need to hunker down like a Missouri mule in a hailstorm and ride it out."

I said, "What does hunker down mean?"

He said, "Hunker down means to dig in. You are probably in a slump because you aren't prospecting enough. You need to dig in and prospect your way out of it."

Then I asked him, "Why is the mule from Missouri?"

He told me that he grew up on a dairy farm in Kansas City and that the mule was the state animal of Missouri. So, of course, the mule was from Missouri.

I said, "We live in California, and I don't know that much about hailstorms. What is a hailstorm?"

He said, "Hail is when rain turns into ice, and a hailstorm typically doesn't last that long, maybe five to fifteen minutes, and then it is over. Just like a sales slump usually doesn't last that long. You aren't going to be **exactly** like a mule and just ride out the hailstorm. What you need to do is hunker down and **prospect your way out** of your sales slump."

I have had many sales slumps in my career. Whenever I get in one, I tell myself, "Steve, you need to hunker down like a Missouri mule in a hailstorm and prospect your way out of it." Over time, the self-talk got shortened to simply hunker down. I also began to realize that hunker down applied to a lot of other situations. When I was procrastinating something, I would say things like: Steve, hunker down and get that proposal done. Steve, hunker down and build your list of prospects for this week. Steve, hunker down, pick up the phone, and make some calls. Hunker down and dig into whatever you need to get done.

**Hunker down.**

# TIP #11

# I can do it, I can do it, if I put my mind to it!

In my first ten years in sales, I made 120,000 calls and conducted 5,000 face-to-face meetings. My daily goal was to make fifty calls. If I did that, I would talk to seventeen prospects, and from that I would set two meetings. When I looked at my numbers, I realized that from the age of 22-32 I was failing 96% of the time to succeed 4% of the time. I did this consistently for about 2,440 working days in a row. At the same time, I was putting 40,000 miles per year on my car in LA traffic. It was quite the galvanizing gauntlet to go through, let me tell you.

I was basically failing forty-eight times a day, and I had to figure out a way to stay motivated despite all of the voicemails, gatekeepers, put-offs, objections, unreturned calls, etc. That was the genesis of: I can do it, I can do it, if I put my mind to it! I had to keep telling myself all day long there was a way to achieve my daily goal of fifty calls while getting it handed to me forty-eight times per day. So, I posted my daily goal of fifty calls on a 3 x 5 card in front of me so I could see it all day long. Whenever I began to lose my enthusiasm or focus, I would look at that 3 x 5 card and say to myself, "I can do it, I can do it, if I put my mind to it!"

One of the most common attributes of high achieving salespeople is they **set a daily prospecting goal**. They then remain focused on achieving that goal through the way that they talk to themselves all day long. Like Henry Ford said, "Whether you think you can or think you can't, you're right." When you're talking to yourself, you're also listening to yourself. You might as well get into the habit of telling yourself **you can** hit your daily goal. Sooner or later, you're going to believe it. If you believe it, you can achieve it.

Every morning, put your prospecting goal in a place you can see it. Throughout the day, tell yourself, "I can do it, I can do it, if I put my mind to it!"

**I can do it, I can do it, if I put my mind to it!**

# TIP #12

# Keep smiling and dialing!

Smiling affects your voice tone and makes it sound more positive and friendly. **A positive attitude is contagious.** Here is how to set the tone for every call you make. The 7-38-55 rule of communication is a concept that came from a study on how we communicate. The rule states that 7% of what we communicate is what we say, 38% of what we communicate is how we say it, and 55% of what we communicate is through our body language. So, when you are making calls, the only things you have got going for you are what you say and how you say it.

Simply put, the single biggest determinant of how you communicate over the phone is your voice, so your tone really matters. If I was in my office from 8:00 am to 5:00 pm, I would block out two to three call blitzes per day, and I would want my voice tone to be just as fresh at 4:30 in the afternoon as it was at 8:30 in the morning. When I mean fresh, I mean I had the same enthusiasm in my voice the entire day. **Enthusiasm sells.** You need a spark to light a fire. You can have the best script in the world, but if you don't say it with enthusiasm, it could whip the prospect into a nap on the other end of the line. You can have the worst script in the world spoken with enthusiasm, and it could work.

That was the origin of the phrase "keep smiling and dialing." Because the act of smiling can impact how you feel, and I needed to feel enthusiastic all day long and have that enthusiasm come through in my voice tone. So I would start my first call blitz of the day with, "Steve, start smiling and dialing." I would start my second call blitz of the day with "Steve, keep smiling and dialing." My last call blitz of the day was, "Steve, just keep on smiling and dialing."

I found that I was actually smiling when I said, "Keep smiling and dialing." It kept me motivated, helping me to have enthusiasm in my voice tone all day long and to achieve my goals. I realize that nobody dials a phone anymore, but the concept still works. All day, every day when prospecting, tell yourself to keep smiling and dialing.

**Keep smiling and dialing.**

# TIP #13

# Selling is a numbers game. In order to win, pick up the phone and dial again.

**M**y sales manager walked through the bullpen one morning chanting, "Selling is a numbers game, and in order to win, pick up the phone and dial it again." I think he did that because he heard crickets that morning instead of the buzz of his sales team prospecting. It was kind of catchy the way he said it. Selling is a numbers game, and in order to win, pick up the phone and dial it again. I liked it. I began to say it over and over to myself and realized that elements of it were true.

Selling is a game. It is a contact sport, and more contact is typically better than less contact. The more you play the game, the better you can get at the game, especially if you are a student of the game and work on your game to become more skilled while playing the game. The beauty of this affirmation is that you can control how many prospecting attempts you make every day, and you are **100% responsible** for your own skill development. If you play the game well, you will generate opportunities for yourself. If you are highly skilled, you will win more than your fair share of those opportunities. In summary, you will win the game.

It's not about the harder you work the luckier you get, even though sometimes that happens, which is great for you! It's about playing the game, realizing it is a contact sport. You learn as you play. You reflect on what worked and didn't work. You adjust, practice, and refine your skills, and you put yourself in a better position to win the game.

Before every call blitz, tell yourself that selling is a numbers game and in order to win you should pick up the phone and dial it again.

**Selling is a numbers game. In order to win, pick up the phone and dial again.**

# TIP #14

# Some will, some won't, so what! Next! Dial another number.

When prospecting, you will encounter a wide variety of gatekeepers and prospects. Some are going to be easy to deal with, and others are going to be tougher than a two-dollar steak. The easy ones and the difficult ones are sometimes not as hard on you emotionally as the ones that are disrespectful and might even hang up on you. These are the situations that can really make you recoil and stop prospecting, which limits your ability to hit your goals. When this happened to me, I had to figure out a way to put this type of rejection into its proper perspective. After an unpleasant interaction like that, the phone looked like it weighed fifty pounds, and I needed to be a 300-pound silverback gorilla on steroids to pick it up.

I created a moniker for these types of people that I felt were impolite, and it was Dirty Shirt McNasty. Whenever I encountered one, I said to myself, "Well, there is another Dirty Shirt McNasty." Then I had to come up with a way to put an umbrella over my head and let the unjust treatment from Dirty Shirt McNasty roll off the top of the umbrella and down my back without affecting me emotionally. That is how "Some will, some won't, so what! Next! Dial another number" came into effect. Whenever I encountered Dirty Shirt McNasty, I would tell myself, "Steve, some will, some won't, so what! Next! Dial another number."

The reason why you say dial another number to yourself after you say, "Some will, some won't, so what! Next!" is that **anything can happen**. You just have to keep moving. You never know what is going to happen on the next call. The average "no" isn't that big of a deal, but an interaction with Dirty Shirt McNasty can bring a call blitz to a screeching halt. Whenever you're prospecting and you encounter Dirty Shirt McNasty, tell yourself, "Some will, some won't, so what! Next! Dial another number."

**Some will, some won't, so what! Next! Dial another number.**

# TIP #15

# Stop stalling and start calling!

When you're prospecting and encountering all of the challenges that come with it, sometimes you can rationalize your priorities and your behavior. You might want to revisit your priorities if you try to squeeze in prospecting around everything else, as opposed to blocking prospecting in the calendar first and squeezing in everything else around that. The reason you are probably doing that is to try to avoid hearing the word no. It's not that no breaks your back — it's your emotional reaction to the word no.

Early on in my career, there were times where I found myself doing things in golden selling time, like building my list, organizing my desk, or talking to my co-workers. You've probably never done any of those things before instead of prospecting. I had to come up with a way to redirect myself from majoring in the minors, and that was where "stop stalling and start calling!" came in.

I would be sitting in my cubicle doing something other than making calls and would say to myself, "Steve, stop stalling and start calling!" Throughout the day, it would sound something like this:

"Steve, I mean, really. Is building your list right now the most important thing you should be doing, or is making calls more important? Stop stalling and start calling! You should have had your list ready before you got in."

"Steve, I mean, really. Is organizing your desk right now the most important thing you should be doing, or is making calls more important? Stop stalling and start calling!"

"Steve, I mean, really. Is talking to your co-workers right now more important than making calls? Stop stalling and start calling! They aren't even prospects. They are suspects!"

Time-block daily call blitzes into your calendar first and work everything else around that. If you find yourself majoring in the minors and not making your calls, you need to redirect your behavior by telling yourself, "Stop stalling and start calling!"

**Stop stalling and start calling.**

# TIP #16

# Make five more calls before five!

Finishing strong is having the determination to see it through to the end. The winner of any competition always comes from among those who finish. Here is how to finish every day strong in sales. My sales manager told me early on that yesterday was a canceled check, tomorrow is a promissory note, but today is cash money. Today is all you have, so you better spend your time wisely. Everyday matters because, if you don't plant a seed today, thirty, sixty or ninety days later it is the calm before the calm. Nothing happens. You gotta make everyday matter. Be true to yourself.

I lived twenty-eight miles away from the office and, depending on what time I got done working, it could take forty-five to ninety minutes to get home. Sometimes I would walk over to the window at 3:30 to see how traffic was shaping up and could see cars getting on the freeway. I wanted to leave so badly and beat the traffic, but I remembered what my sales manager told me, to be true to myself. So, I began to say to myself at the end of the day, "Steve, make five more calls before five. **End in victory.** All you have to do to make that happen is to make five more calls before five. Steve, what harm is going to come from you making 25 more calls this week, 100 more calls this month, and 1,200 more calls by the end of the year? But right now, all you need to do is make five more calls before five."

There are many ways to prospect, calls, emails, texts, LinkedIn, networking events, etc., but the same principle still applies. It does not necessarily need to be a call; it is merely five more prospecting attempts before five o'clock. If you want to end in victory and be true to yourself before you decide to leave for the day, tell yourself, "Make five more calls before five."

**Make five more calls before five!**

# TIP #17

# You poor little thing. Do you want your mommy?

Working on a straight commission my entire career, I have had some bad days, bad weeks, and sales slumps. Some resulted in too much month at the end of the money, no paycheck, and putting everything on a credit card until next month. Then the next month everything I had been working on came in, and I had a huge month and would pay it all off and pull a little bit ahead financially. I learned the importance of sticking to the fundamentals and putting prospects in the top end of my pipeline consistently, every day, because the quality and quantity of what goes in is ultimately what comes out. The majority of the time, when prospects move forward, it will happen in their timeframe, not yours. This sometimes coincides with the peaks and valleys of when things land and the fluctuations in the size of your commission checks.

I was at a regional sales meeting, and a speaker was telling us all about his highs and lows as a salesperson. I could really identify with what he said, because even though he was very consistent with his prospecting efforts, his paycheck was very inconsistent. It almost drove him out of the business a few times. He then told us the self-talk he used when the situation got very dire. He said he didn't have to do it that many times, but when he did, it worked. It's called the bathroom talk. He said it was only to be used so you don't take yourself too seriously and to level set yourself. Everything will be okay if you just **stay the course**.

He told us, "Here is what you do. Walk into the bathroom, put your hands on the counter, look into the mirror and say, 'You poor little thing. Do you want your mommy?' If that doesn't put a smile on your face, what will? Then go back into your office and make more calls, because everything is going to be okay."

If things get bad, your pipeline is running dry, and the situation looks grim, walk into the bathroom, put your hands on the counter, look into the mirror and say, "You poor little thing. Do you want your mommy?"

**"You poor little thing. Do you want your mommy?"**

# TIP #18

# I'm terrific, I'm tremendous, and when I close, I'm stupendous!

One day, my manager and I were getting ready for a meeting with a big prospect. My manager told me that I needed to have the right mindset prior to going into any meeting. When I asked him how, he said, "You do this by creating an expectation of a positive outcome. The way you do that is by what you say to yourself before you go in."

I said, "Well, what should I say?"

He said, "I'm terrific, I'm tremendous, and when I close, I'm stupendous." It was awesome. I loved it!

So we said, "I'm terrific, I'm tremendous, and when I close, I'm stupendous," three times together in that underground parking garage on 7th and Figueroa. After that, we went into the meeting and fortunately were able to land the opportunity.

I have sold over $60,000,000 of sales training in my career and have said "I'm terrific, I'm tremendous, and when I close, I'm stupendous" more times than I can count. In garages, elevator banks, walking off planes. I have come up short many times, but it has never failed to put a smile on my face walking into a meeting.

We all have the emotional intelligence to know that we are not really closing the sale. If there is a good fit, we are just asking the prospect if they are willing to take to the next step with us.

Before your next meeting, tell yourself, "I'm terrific, I'm tremendous, and when I close, I'm stupendous."

**I'm terrific, I'm tremendous, and when I close, I'm stupendous.**

# TIP #19

# Don't get bitter get better.

R ejection can be tough to take, and it can have an impact on our attitude. You can get frustrated, take things personally, or even get defensive. My sales manager told me that you must take complete and total responsibility and ownership when you lose a sales opportunity. You can self-reflect by conducting a sales autopsy.

I asked, "How do I do that?"

He said, "Ask yourself questions like, Was I prepared? Did I ask the right questions? Was the prospect the decision maker? Did I oversell? Was I talking too much and not listening? Don't go to that dark place whenever you lose a sale and start placing blame elsewhere by saying things like, 'They weren't qualified anyway. They just could not see our value add. They already knew who they were going to go with. They weren't the decision maker anyway. Our price is too high! Our products and services aren't competitive, etc.'"

My sales manager reminded me that the problem lies not in the stars but within myself. He told me don't get bitter get better! This advice was so beneficial, **avoid blaming**, don't get bitter get better. After every meeting held, conduct a sales autopsy to determine what went well and see if there were any opportunities for improvement. If you come up short like I have done many times, tell yourself, "Don't get bitter get better." Then begin closing your skill gaps with practice.

**Don't get bitter get better.**

# TIP #20

# If you're not out selling, you're being outsold!

I was always concerned about my competition. I did not fear any of them, but I respected them. Because I was on straight commission, I was always worried that, if they were able to take some of my clients away from me, my income and livelihood would be significantly impacted.

I remember saying things to myself about my competition like this:

- Are they prospecting my clients?
- Are they better prepared?
- Do they follow up better?
- Are they outworking me?

This became the start of the genesis of the phrase "If you're not out selling, you're being outsold." As I was thinking these thoughts about my competition, I would say to myself, "If you're not out selling, you're being outsold." I concluded that **the only thing I could control was myself** – my attitude and my effort. I decided to become more proactive in my approach to not only, retain my client, but to do more business with them.

So, what did I do? I developed the deepest understanding of my products and services that I could. I prepared better for every meeting. I listened better at every meeting. I improved my presentation skills. I did what I said I was going to do, when I said I was going to do it. I under promised and over delivered. I made every possible effort I could to add more value to my clients than I ever did before. I had the steely resolve that my competition would never out-hustle me.

In modern day terminology, I had productive paranoia. I began thinking about every possible worst-case scenario that would come out of my competition taking my clients from me. I took the time to consider what I could do to make sure I didn't lose clients to my competition. As a result, I became more disciplined in my approach with my clients.

I needed my value to be perceived by my clients as far more than the products and services I was selling. That I was the differentiating factor. My commitment to them further developed their trust in me.

If you are concerned about your competition, as you should be, tell yourself, "If you're not out selling, you're being outsold." Then reflect on the true value that you believe you are adding to your clients. If you feel you have some holes in your game, make some adjustments and develop more rigor in your routine as a salesperson. Add more value to your clients than the competition ever could.

**If you're not out selling, you're being outsold.**

# TIP #21

# Don't take rejection personally.

On my very first day in sales, my goal was to make one hundred calls. It was a rough day. I made ninety calls, no contacts, no appointments, rough time with gatekeepers, and voicemail was just coming out, if you can believe it. I remember that my name was going on a pink slip of paper that read, "While you were out." I even had a blister on the end of my finger. By the end of the day, I was dialing with the eraser tip of my #2 Trusty pencil.

It was the worst day of my life. I said to myself that I'd made a mistake getting into sales. My head was down when my sales manager came to my desk.

He said to me, "Do you know how many times Babe Ruth struck out?"

I said, "I don't know, and I don't care. I think that I made a serious mistake in my career selection. I am not cut out for this type of rejection."

He said, "Do you know how many times Babe Ruth hit a home run?"

I said, "714."

He said, "Babe Ruth struck out 1330 times, but he also hit 714 home runs. In sales, no one cares about how many times you strike out. They only care about how many times you hit a home run. The number of home runs you hit is in direct proportion to the number of times you strikeout, so develop the ability to get back up there and keep swinging."

From that point on, I came to realize that not every prospect wanted or needed what I sold. What I started focusing on were the ones that did. Rejection was part of the game, and I accepted it and put it in its proper perspective. Point being, I expected rejection and didn't take it personally. When I didn't take it personally and moved past it, I was able to keep calling and finish my call blitz.

Here are a few key points to help you to not take rejection personally.

1. **Use positive self-talk** to help you rebound from rejection and keep yourself focused and motivated to continue prospecting.

2. **Be understanding** of their situation. Remember, you are an interruption in their day. Sometimes, they pick up the phone when they are busy and their emotional reaction to you can be rather abrupt. They may come off as being rude or impolite. Make an allowance for their behavior, and don't take it personally.

3. **Shake it off.** Pick up the phone and make another call. The very next call could be to someone who wants or needs what you are selling.

**Don't take rejection personally.**

# TIP #22

# Reverse engineer your prospecting numbers.

I was always looking for ways to get and stay motivated, so one day I decided to reverse engineer my prospecting numbers to determine exactly how much money I was making doing the activity I did the most, which was dial a phone. I discovered I was making about $10 dollars per dial. I realized that every time I touched the phone, I was making money, and my mindset changed about prospecting. I looked at my phone, and it transformed itself before my eyes, and it began to look like a cash register. No matter what happened on the other end of the line, every time I made a call, I was making $10. I was able to associate touching the phone with making money. I could not have gotten there without tracking and reverse engineering my numbers. It was a game changer for me because it got me into the **art of painless prospecting**. Try it. It could work for you too.

If you would like to hear what the Tips in Part I sound like, go to our YouTube channel and click on the Playlist "Using Positive Self-Talk to Impact Your Prospecting Mindset."

**https://www.youtube.com/@NextLevelSalesConsulting/playlists**

# PART II

# PROSPECTING FOCUS

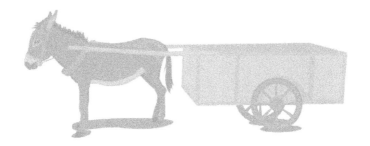

# CHAPTER 1

# HAVE A TARGET MARKET

# TIP 23

# Don't be all things to all people; be all things to a select few.

After I left Dale Carnegie and started my own business, I was a generalist—I worked with a variety of companies in different industries. I took on every client I could because I had to get the business off the ground. One day I would be working on AT&T, the next day Enterprise Rent-A-Car, and on the third day the Los Angeles Dodgers. I had to create a new program every time I landed a new client, and when I came up against a competitor that was more of a specialist in that target market, it made winning the business more challenging. I lost an opportunity with a big prospect that stung. I thought we had a good value proposition, but they went with a competitor that had more experience working in that target market. It was a good old-fashioned bake off, and I suffered a good, old-fashioned country ass-whippin'.

So, I decided to make a change. Instead of being a generalist, I would become a specialist. I decided to **go narrow and deep** in a target market. Instead of being a little bit to everybody and nothing to anybody, I wanted to be all things to a select few.

I made the decision to specialize in a target market. As a result, our strategy changed with our:

- Prospecting focus
- Branding
- Website
- Marketing collateral
- LinkedIn activity
- YouTube channel

In addition, I began to say no to opportunities that were not in my target market. After those changes were made, over time I noticed several things.

1. I was better able to source prospects and **develop marketing messages** that are customized to the target. We use that messaging on our website, LinkedIn profile, and when sponsoring industry events. In our marketing materials, we are able to brand and credential ourselves to that target market by providing a list of our current clients and our capabilities.

2. I continued to **gain more experience** with the target market, which increased my knowledge, credibility, and expertise. I don't know everything there is to know about the target market, but I learn more every day. We have built a reputation as a resource in the target market and a thought leader in the industry. This has helped us to generate more opportunities. Prospects trust our opinion. We have street cred.

3. Because we understand our target market, we **add more value** to our clients as specialists than if they were to work with a generalist, saving them time and money.

4. We **differentiate ourselves** and highlight our uniqueness against our competition. When we are trying to win an opportunity and are up against a generalist, we have a distinct advantage.

5. It has helped us to **maximize referrals and personal introductions** in our target market.

It is hard to grow with a high degree of velocity when you try to be all things to all people. It creates inefficiencies in your business. If you are a generalist, consider evolving into a specialist. Over the long haul, it is easier and more profitable to be narrow and deep and all things to a select few.

What to do? Think about becoming a specialist instead of a generalist. Determine a target market to focus on where you can go narrow and deep.

# TIP 24

# Build your ideal client profile.

When prospecting, you want to have a target market and, within that target market, have a defined ideal client profile to help you focus your prospecting activities. The more specific you are, the better.

So, what is an ideal client profile? Simply put, it is the kind of client you want. It is a profile that you create that highlights the attributes of your prospects so that you can better identify them and target them with your prospecting efforts. This can take shape in the type of company or individual prospect you want to work with. One of the first steps in being successful at prospecting is to be focused. There is nothing that creates focus better than having clarity on exactly who you want to work with.

How do you create the ideal client profile? The way I did this was simple. I took an inventory of my best clients and wrote down the attributes they all had in common. I then prioritized those **attributes** to help me to develop more **clarity** on them. For example, it was a wealth management company with five hundred or more salespeople, in a growth mode, willing to invest in training and development, and open to working with somebody from the outside.

What is the benefit of defining your ideal client profile? What I found was that I was more focused with my prospecting efforts, could customize my approach better, and was able to gain more referrals that fit my ideal client profile.

From my experience, one of the most important elements of a successful relationship is the fit. The ideal client profile can be best described as the **best fit** companies and individuals for you to work with.

What to do? Make a list of your ten best clients and determine the common attributes they possess. Then create your ideal client profile.

# TIP 25

# Stay on the pulse of your target market.

**A**s you focus on your target market and your ideal prospect, you want to learn as much as possible about them. You also want to keep up to date with what's happening in your target market. Here are some examples of ways you can do this:

- Subscribe to Google Alerts.
- Subscribe to LinkedIn Sales Navigator.
- Search LinkedIn for local groups and information.
- Go to their company websites.
- Attend the events they go to.

Staying on the pulse of your target market will enable you to follow the trends in the industry. You can customize and personalize your communications. It enables you to engage with your prospects in a more meaningful way, connecting with them through timely and relevant outreach.

What to do? Make a list of the things you can do to stay on the pulse of your target market.

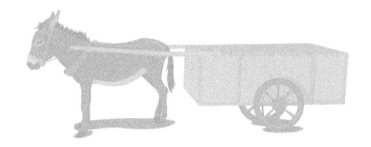

## CHAPTER 2

# GET YOUR MESSAGING DOWN

# TIP 26

# How to create your
# value proposition.

N ow that you have identified your target market and ideal prospect, you will want to put yourself in situations where you will be able to communicate your customized value proposition to your prospects.

A value proposition explains the benefit you provide, who you provide it to, and how you do it uniquely, in one brief sentence. It describes your target market, the pain points you solve, and how they benefit. It would sound like this: We help (target market) with (situation) so that they can (benefit).

You would typically use your value proposition on an outbound call, in a voicemail, at a networking event or in any interaction with anyone who could possibly be a prospect. This should take no more than five to ten seconds.

Here are some examples we use:

- We help financial services firms improve advisor productivity so they can gain more market share.
- We help professional sports teams sell out every game, every night, so they can maximize their per-game revenue.
- We help banks bring their full value proposition to their clients so they can meet all their clients' financial needs.

The bottom line is that you want to be prepared with a few different value propositions for **each of your target markets**. Unlike the elevator speech or elevator pitch (tips #24 & #25), which could be predicated on someone asking you what you do, you can use your value proposition anytime, anywhere.

What to do? Use this simple formula: We help (target market) with (situation) so that they can (benefit). Then create your value propositions for your target markets.

# TIP 27

# How to create your elevator speech.

Y ou may find yourself in situations where you may want to use a broader version of your value proposition to customize your messaging to your prospects. We call this an elevator speech.

So, what is an elevator speech? It is a thirty-second commercial that communicates a lot of things in a brief amount of time—the time it takes to ride the elevator from the top of a building to the bottom. The concept behind the elevator speech is that you can give it to **anyone, anywhere, at any time**, particularly if someone asks you what you do. The purpose of your elevator speech is to motivate them to want to hear or learn more. It should be no longer than thirty seconds, eighty to ninety words or eight to ten sentences.

The elevator speech can be used in any situation. Here is how it goes:

- Start with your introduction: My name is (your name), and I am (state your role), with (company name).
- Then give your value proposition: What we do is help (target market) with (situation) so that they can (benefit).
- Then explain how you do it: We do this by (state your process).
- Then explain how you are different: We are different by (state your uniqueness).
- Then end with a call to action or a question, depending on the situation.

It might sound something like this:

My name is Steve Johnson, and I am the president of The Next Level Sales Consulting. We help financial services firms increase the productivity of their Financial Advisors so that they can grow their business and gain more market share. We do this by gathering the best practices of their most productive financial advisors then train and coach their new hires to execute those best practices. We are different because we have trained and coached over 20,000 financial advisors in the last twenty years, more than anybody in the business. Thanks for asking. What do you do for work?

In summary, an elevator speech is a clear, brief message about who you are, what you do, how you do it, who you do it for, and how they benefit, ending with a call to action or question.

What to do? Create your elevator speech using this format as a resource.

# TIP 28

# How to create your elevator pitch.

The elevator speech is used in any situation. The elevator pitch is used in a sales situation. So how do you turn your elevator speech into an elevator pitch? There are a variety of ways to do this, but one of the most common ways is through asking a question based on a need. When you are in a sales setting and someone asks what you do, you will simply grab their attention by asking a question that focuses on a problem they may have or a problem that you help to solve. You will answer their question initially by asking them a brief question. For example, when they ask you what you do, it might sound something like this.

- Thanks for asking. Just out of curiosity, is bringing in new priority households one of your goals?
- Thanks for asking. Just out of curiosity, is improving the retention rates of your three-year-and-under financial advisors one of your goals?
- Thanks for asking. Just out of curiosity, is bringing the full value proposition of your firm to your clients and gaining more wallet share one of your goals?

After they respond to the question, you will want to customize your elevator pitch based on their response. I say something like:

I'm Steve Johnson, the president of The Next Level Sales Consulting. We help financial services firms like Merrill Lynch, Morgan Stanley, and Raymond James retain and increase the productivity of their financial advisors so that they can grow their business and gain more market share. We do this by gathering the best practices of their most productive financial advisors and transferring those best practices to others. We are different because we have trained and coached over 20,000 financial advisors in the last twenty years, more than anybody in the business. Thanks for asking. What brought you to the event today?

In summary, an elevator pitch is a clear, brief message about who you are, what you do, how you do it, who you do it for, and how they benefit, ending with a call to action or question. You will preface your elevator pitch with a question based on a need by asking a question that focuses on a problem they may have or a problem that you help to solve.

What to do? Think about all the places you go where your clients and prospects get together. Think about the problems they may need solved. Come up with a few questions that might spark curiosity if they ask you what it is you do. Then deliver your elevator pitch and let them know that you can solve those problems.

# TIP 29

# How to answer, "What got you into that?" with your why.

After you communicate your value proposition, it is not uncommon for the person you are speaking with to ask you a follow-up question, such as "How did you get into that business?" or "What got you into that?" These questions give you an opportunity to state your **why**—why you got into what you are doing. This is your opportunity to tell your story.

What you do is very important. But **why** you do what you do is what is most compelling to other people. It's important for you to be able to communicate your **why,** because that is where the emotional connection happens. People don't buy what you do, they buy **why** you do it. When you can communicate your **why,** your purpose behind the **why** comes through. You do this by telling your story. People always ask me how I got into the business, and this is what I say,

> My parents owned and operated the Dale Carnegie training franchise in Los Angeles for thirty years. When I graduated college, I took the Dale Carnegie public speaking course. At twenty-two, I was the youngest person there, with forty corporate executives. Over the twelve weeks of the program, I saw many of my classmates conquer their fear of public speaking. For many people in the program, it was a game changer for building self-confidence. When the class was over, my dad asked me if I was interested in coming to work for him, and I said I was twenty-two years old and had never sold anything, but I could get behind that. I got into the training business because I could see the difference it made in people's lives.

What to do? Think of how you can communicate your **why.** What is your story? When someone asks you what you do and follows up by asking how you got into that, be ready to tell them your **why** to create that emotional connection.

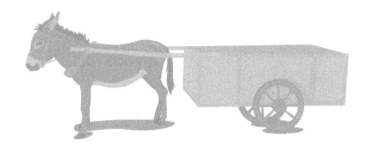

# CHAPTER 3

# MAXIMIZE YOUR TIME: GETTING READY TO PROSPECT

# TIP 30

# Why sourcing prospects consistently is important.

It's important to consistently build and refine your prospect list. In order to do this, you need to time block two activities into your calendar consistently. One activity is the time to source and refine your prospect list, and the other activity is to prospect that list. I can't tell you the countless thousands of hours I have spent in the last thirty-eight+ years building a list of prospects to reach out to.

What I discovered over the course of my career is that many people in sales run out of prospects to contact because they don't spend enough time sourcing. Much like painting a house, you spend a lot of time doing prep work – stripping off old paint, sanding rough spots, repairing damaged areas, caulking the trim, etc. Once all that preparation is complete, the actual painting of the house takes much less time. The same thing happens in prospecting – you have to spend time doing the legwork upfront finding names, researching those names, and building your list. Then you can begin prospecting.

The first thing I do is set a goal each week for the number of prospects I want to source that week. Then I get on LinkedIn, use the advanced search filters to look for accounts and leads that fit my ideal client profile, and I continue building my list. Once I identify leads, I look to see if I have any common connections that can arrange a personal introduction. I then go to the company websites to confirm the information is accurate and up to date.

These are just two things I do to source prospects. There are many other ways to build your list. I do these activities in a time block on Friday to build my list of prospects to contact the following Monday.

What to do? Determine the best way for you to source a list of prospects that fit your ideal client profile, then block time in your calendar for sourcing.

# TIP 31

# Research prospects to customize your approach.

The old spray and pray technique of prospecting is out, and customizing your prospecting approach so that it resonates with the prospect is in. This works best because your prospecting outreach will be timely and relevant. Here is how I use LinkedIn to conduct my research on a prospect that I think is a good fit for what we do.

I focus on these four areas of their profile:

- **Experience at their current job:** This lets me know if they are a decision-maker or an influencer in their company.
- **Experience at their former jobs**: This lets me know their experience in the industry and any possible shared connections at their prior employment.
- **Mutual connections:** This is where I look for a familiar name that I can contact to learn more about the prospect or potentially ask for a personal introduction to the prospect.
- **Recent activity**: I look at their activity to gauge the pulse of where their interests are focused. The most interesting activity I like to see is when they are generating personal posts and not just company or industry-related thought leadership.

Based on this research, I am better able to personalize and customize my approach to prospects I have identified that fit my ideal client profile. Based on the results of my research, I then determine the best way to contact the prospect (email, personal introduction, phone call, LinkedIn connection request, etc.)

What to do? Once you have a list of prospects to contact, block time in your calendar for researching those prospects and then determine the best approach to contact each one.

# TIP 32

# Make suspecting calls to identify the decision maker.

When I am developing my list and cross-referencing LinkedIn to a company website, there are certain situations when I'm not sure that the name I sourced is the correct decision maker. For what we do, selling business to business, it's critical that we engage with the decision maker, because they are the ones who can truly say yes. If I am selling to non-decision makers, they can say no, but they can't say yes. This sounds really old-school, but picking up the phone is oftentimes the best way for me to determine who the decision maker is. I call this the suspecting call.

A key ally on a suspecting call, to help you determine who the decision maker is, is the gatekeeper. They are typically an executive assistant or associate who has direct contact with the decision maker. It is challenging to connect with a decision maker without connecting with a gatekeeper first. When speaking with the gatekeeper, you can ask them questions, and they can point you in the right direction. They can help you confirm or identify the decision maker.

Here are a couple examples:

- I need your help. We work with companies on sales force effectiveness projects. Who in your company oversees sales and is responsible for improving the performance of the entire sales team?
- I need your help. We work with call centers like AT&T on sales force effectiveness projects to improve conversion rates. Is (name) responsible for your call centers? (If not) Who is?

What to do? If you need to confirm or determine who the decision maker is, make a suspecting call, interact with the gatekeeper, and ask some qualifying questions.

# TIP 33

# Use a checklist to maximize your prospecting time blocks.

O nce you have built your list and conducted research on your prospects, it's time to contact them. The way I maximize my prospecting efforts is to go through a checklist, which requires planning and preparation. Here is the checklist I go through to get ready for a time block of prospecting.

1. Have contact information ready: prospect's name, work and cell #s, email address.
2. Review notes on any prior interactions with the prospect.
3. Review research to personalize the interaction.
4. Establish a goal for the outreach. What am I trying to accomplish?
5. If it is a cold call, how I am going to use my research to make it a warm call.
6. Customize my value proposition to the prospect.
7. Prepare a short list of the questions to ask.
8. Anticipate any objections the prospect may have and have some responses ready.
9. Prepare any information they might request.
10. Have my calendar ready with specific dates and times to schedule a meeting.

The bottom line to maximizing the productivity of your prospecting time blocks is to develop and use a checklist to help you get ready to prospect.

What to do? Use this checklist as a template to prepare your own in order to maximize your prospecting time blocks.

# TIP 34

# Use multiple communication modalities when prospecting.

When I am in a prospecting time block, I use multiple communication modalities and bundle those activities together. The best approach is a blended approach with multiple modalities of communication. The benefit of this strategy is that the chance of you connecting with your prospect may be greater when you appeal to their preferred communication style. As you know, you will catch more fish with a net than a single line.

I bundle my prospecting activities and do them at the same time. For example, if I send a connection request on LinkedIn, I back it up with a phone call and, if I can't connect, back it up with a voicemail. If I leave a voicemail for a prospect, I back it up with an email. If I send an email, I back it up with a phone call. Remember, **it's a contact sport**. Multiple modalities of communication are the way to go.

My most common initial outreaches are with LinkedIn, email, and phone. Once I am engaged with the prospect, I broaden the communication modalities I utilize to stay engaged with them. The primary ones are texting (but don't overdo it), attending networking events, conferences, or trade shows where I know they are going to be.

What to do? Bundle your prospecting activities together. You can't go wrong with multiple communication modalities with prospects. It will improve your level of visibility, which will increase the odds of you being top of mind when they have a need.

# TIP 35

# It doesn't matter how you prospect; it only matters that you prospect.

I n addition to using multiple communication modalities, you want to use multiple prospecting tactics to engage with prospects in your target market. Why is that? Because everything works and nothing works. From my experience, it will take eight touches to get an opportunity going. Prospects are a moving target, so use as many different tactics as you can. **A blended prospecting approach is the best approach.**

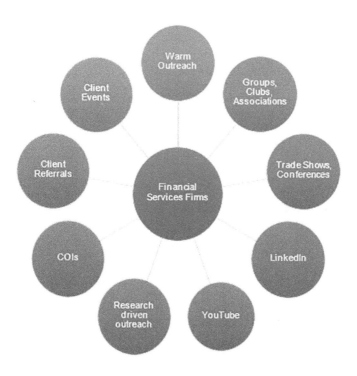

For example, for our target market, I will make a warm outreach. I will sponsor, attend, and/or speak at groups, clubs, associations, trade shows, and conferences they attend. I leverage LinkedIn to post thought leadership, connect with prospects, and invite them to go to our YouTube channel. I turn cold calls into research driven outreach. I form referral alliances with COIs, and we introduce each other to prospects. I ask my clients for referrals and personal introductions. I do client recognition events.

One way I engage with prospects is to share content that may pique their interest in meeting with us. We consistently look for ways to engage with prospects to develop and build a relationship with them.

Simply put, it doesn't matter how you prospect. It only matters that you prospect. The best approach is a combination of prospecting tactics that creates the eight touches.

What to do? Try everything. Then, through trial and error, determine what works and doesn't work. Then do more of what works and less of what doesn't work.

# TIP 36

# Take notes when prospecting.

**W**hile you are prospecting, it's important to take notes. **The faintest ink is more powerful than the strongest memory.** Be ready to take notes. While I'm prospecting, I document important information that I uncover throughout the conversation. I look to uncover what they want to accomplish, their motives, timeframes, budget, who else is part of the decision-making process, their openness to working with a consulting firm, etc. Literally, I write down every piece of information that might be important enough to help me win the opportunity.

These notes help me to summarize the conversations in a follow up email if needed, and I will use those notes in the future to anchor back to prior conversations. I use the same principle when in conversation with my clients, documenting things like where they went to college, their career path, what they like to do when they are not working, and their kids' interests. Doing this with both prospects and clients helps me to further build rapport and establish common ground when in conversation.

What to do? Prepare to take detailed notes on every interaction with prospects. Then use those notes to follow-up, set next steps, and create customized proposals and recommendations.

# TIP 37

# Practice your prospecting skills.

Rejection can be tough to take, and it can have an impact on our attitude. You can get frustrated, take things personally, or even get defensive. My sales manager told me that I must take complete and total responsibility and ownership when I lost a sales opportunity. He told me to self-reflect.

I asked, "How do I do that?"

He said, "Ask yourself questions. Was I prepared? Did I ask the right questions? Was the prospect the decision maker? Did I oversell? Was I talking too much and not listening?"

He told me not to go to that dark place whenever I came up short. Don't start the blame game by saying things like:

- They weren't qualified anyway.
- They just could not see our value add.
- They already knew who they were going to go with.
- They weren't the decision maker anyway.
- Our price is too high.

My sales manager reminded me that the problem lies not in the stars but within myself. He told me, don't get bitter, get better! So, I asked how I could get better. He said to practice! I asked how I should practice.

He said, "Practice every day for fifteen minutes right before you start prospecting." I am going to share with you the three steps he told me to do.

1.  **Practice one prospecting skill at a time**. For example, I knew that when calling corporate executives, I was going to get the objection, "I'm too busy to get together" all day long, so I practiced a response over and over before making my calls. I still remember my first response that I practiced so many times:

71

I can understand you're busy. Most successful people are. That is why they like to meet for breakfast before the day gets going. How about we get together for breakfast one day next week? I can come to you.

2. **Practice slowly then pick up your pace.** Especially when you are practicing a script and really want to get the words down with the right voice tone and inflection. Slower is better.

3. **Practice relentlessly.** In pressure situations, you always fall back on what is most familiar. What you fall back on will typically be what you have practiced the most. When you practice your skills, you will become more confident, and your confidence will manifest itself when it matters most. Under pressure.

This advice was beneficial. Avoid blaming. Don't get bitter, get better. Practice your skills for fifteen minutes before you prospect.

What to do? Prior to prospecting, set aside fifteen minutes to practice.

# TIP 38

# Set a daily prospecting goal.

On my first day in sales, my sales manager told me, "Prospecting is like shaving. Unless you do it every day, you are going to look like a bum." Every day matters. Having a daily goal will enable you to stay focused on the task at hand.

For my first ten years in sales, I had a goal of making fifty calls and setting two meetings per day, and that helped me to measure my progress and hold myself accountable. I realized that today was all I had, and to get the most out of today I had to have a goal. What I learned was that the only thing I could control was myself—my attitude and my effort. Having a daily prospecting goal enabled me to continue to **put prospects in the top end of my sales funnel** (pipeline). Sooner or later, something had to come out of the bottom of the funnel. Another benefit of having that daily goal was that it helped me **cut out distractions**. I found myself sticking to my prospecting plan instead of talking to co-workers.

Having a daily prospecting goal **kept me motivated**, which generated enthusiasm. That enthusiasm manifested itself in my attitude, which came across in my voice tone when speaking with prospects on the other end of the line. Whenever I faced rejection, the daily prospecting goal gave me the motivation to keep going.

Remember, prospecting is like shaving. Unless you do it every day you are going to look like a bum. What to do? Set a prospecting goal every day.

# TIP 39

# Four fundamentals for setting daily prospecting goals.

What I have observed while working with over 90,000 salespeople in the last thirty-eight years is that those who set daily prospecting goals have more enthusiasm. Their goals help keep them focused, and their genuine enthusiasm is a byproduct of that focus. In my opinion, enthusiasm is one of the most highly compensated qualities in sales, mostly because it is the rarest, yet it is the most contagious. **Enthusiasm is the yeast that rises the dough.** Here are four tips for setting daily prospecting goals:

1. Write your goals down.

   - Writing them down helps you to clarify your goals.

2. Put your written goals in places so that you can see them every day.

   - Having them right there in front of you is a constant reminder of what you are trying to accomplish. It also makes it easier to track your progress.

3. Read your goals first thing in the morning, every morning.

   - When you read your goals every morning, they begin to sink into your subconscious mind. Every single day at every opportunity, your subconscious mind is trying to find ways to help you reach your goal.

4.  Break bigger goals down into smaller goals. Then ask yourself, "What am I going to focus on today?"

    •   Having a daily goal will bring a level of prioritization to your day and help you to focus on what really needs to get done.

What to do? Write your goals down, put them where you can see them, and read them every morning. Break bigger goals into smaller goals.

# TIP 40

# Time is your most precious resource – use it purposefully.

One surefire way to reach your goals is to time block your prospecting activities in your calendar. Then have the self-discipline to protect those time blocks at all costs. What matters most must never come second to what matters least. Here are ten time blocking best practices:

1. Divide your day into time blocks.
2. Dedicate each block to a specific activity.
3. Focus on the planned activity – plan your work and work your plan.
4. Make each block a mini deadline with a specific start/stop time and a goal for what you want to achieve.
5. Develop a routine.
6. Block your time the night before. Take the last fifteen to thirty minutes of every day to plan the next day.
7. Try to avoid distractions when working in a time block such as, cell phones/texting, surfing the internet, talking to co-workers, social media, email.
8. Take breaks. Resting is as important as working. Ninety minutes on, thirty minutes off.
9. Be adaptable. No matter how well you plan, things come up. Priorities can shift.

   - Consider the importance and the urgency of the thing that came up before you move out of your time block. Some things can wait until the time block is over. Not everything is urgent and important.

10. Block your time in advance – at the beginning for the week/ month.

- Block your time on Sunday nights or block your time at the beginning of the month.

What to do? Select one of these ten time blocking best practices to implement now.

# TIP 41

# Time block no more
# than half your day.

Time blocking no more than half of my day for prospecting gives me the rest of the day to do everything else. I don't feel over-scheduled and know that when a time block of prospecting is over, I can return calls, return emails, and log my prospecting notes into CRM. Here is an example:

7:30 – 8:00 – Daily LinkedIn routine:
- Ask five people to connect.
- Ask five connections for a meeting.
- Ask one connection for an introduction.

9:00 – 10:00 – Make warm calls to my network to have five contacts.

12:30 – 2:00 – Attend a networking event with a goal of making five quality contacts.

3:00 – 4:00 – Research driven calls to corporate executives with a goal of five contacts.

**Time is your most precious resource.** It is the one thing that nobody has more of than anyone else. Yet, some people are happier, more productive, and more successful than others. This means that your accomplishments are set by the way that you manage your time. One way to manage your time is through time blocking. How you manage your time is the foundation of your effectiveness.

What to do? Time block no more than half your day.

# TIP 42

# Get more done in less time.

Those who are able to get more done in less time are able to prioritize what matters most and work in an efficient and effective manner to live out their priorities. I am a big believer that life is won on the margins and that **a little difference can make a big difference**, especially in how you decide to spend your time. So here are five things that work for me, maybe some of them will work for you too.

1.  **Get an early start.**

    I live in Los Angeles, and what I have learned by getting an early start is that there are fewer people in the gym, less traffic on the freeway, and if I have an early meeting for breakfast there are fewer people in line. I can get everywhere quicker. I can get in and out of the gym faster and won't have to wait in a line for breakfast. I am also less likely to be late to a breakfast meeting because there is less traffic. Bottom line is that there is less competition for resources the earlier you get your day started.

    When I start my day early in the morning, there are fewer distractions, and I can work more proactively on my biggest priority for the day. I can get more done in less time because there is less competition for my time the earlier I start.

2.  **Do the most important thing first.**

    If there is one thing that I have learned, it is that speed matters, especially when it comes to follow up. Oftentimes, the most important task of the day for me is to follow up on opportunities. For example, if I had a meeting late Monday afternoon and need to write either an executive summary or a proposal, that will happen the first thing Tuesday morning. I want the prospect to show up for work on Tuesday with my email sitting in their inbox. I have found that when I treat a prospect like they are already a client while they are still a prospect with the speed of my follow up, they become a client. Speedy follow-up is important. That's why I do it first thing in the morning.

3. **Do the easiest thing first.**

At the end of each day, I write down a list of all the things I want to do the next day. If there is no real pressing priority but a lot of things to do, many times I will start out the day by doing the easiest thing first. After I do that, I get a win under my belt, and I cross the task off my to do list. One thing I say to myself as I am doing this is, "Steve, you are like butter. You are on a roll." I then move down to the next thing to do on the list and keep up my momentum of getting things done, crossing them off one at a time.

4. **Batch similar tasks together.**

When I batch my tasks, I simply put similar tasks together and do them all at once instead of juggling between different tasks. What I have discovered is that many of the things I do require a specific mindset, and once I get into a groove I want to stay in that groove. I typically batch three tasks on a day-to-day basis.

One is my email. I do it three times a day. In the morning, I clear out my inbox and send any emails I need to send. Right before or after lunch, I do the same thing, and at the end of the day I do the same thing. I compose emails better when I get into the mindset of responding or writing one email after the other. I also get them done in less time.

Second is returning and making calls. I write a list of people I want to call, and I don't put the phone down. I make one call right after the other. I am in the mindset of making calls, I get into a rhythm and my pace is good. I am able to make more calls and have quality conversations because I am locked in to making calls.

Third is logging my notes in CRM. While I am making calls, I take notes on a yellow pad. Well-documented notes really matter, especially when preparing for the next conversation with that prospect. After my time block of calls is over, I log all my notes in one shot into CRM. When I'm in the mindset of logging notes in CRM, I get them done faster and better.

**5.  Cut out distractions.**

When I started in sales, I worked in a bullpen, and there were a lot of distractions from my co-workers that impacted my ability to get my two daily call blitzes done. I got tired of being interrupted, so I put up a sign while I was making calls that said, "Please do not disturb. Prospecting in progress." When my call blitz was over, my co-workers knew I was available for a conversation.

Now distraction is more than just me, a phone, and my co-workers. It is email, texting, LinkedIn, Facebook, Twitter, Instagram, YouTube, etc. Distractions are an epidemic, and trying to keep up with them can become an addictive habit. What I do is turn off the alerts, close out the apps, and turn my phone upside down to stay focused.

What to do? Hopefully one of these time management tips resonated with you. The simplicity of what to do is there, but the execution is difficult. Pick one and stay the course.

# TIP 43

# Track your prospecting activity.

I was always looking for ways to get and stay motivated, so one day I decided to reverse engineer my prospecting numbers to determine exactly how much money I was making doing the activity I did the most, which was dial a phone.

I already had the data because I added up my numbers for the year - dials, contacts, meetings held, and my income. I was able to determine how much money a dial, a contact, and a meeting were worth. I focused on how much money a dial was worth, because without that dial there would be no contact or meeting.

I discovered I was making about $10 dollars per dial. When I realized that, every time I touched the phone, I was making money, my mindset changed about prospecting. I looked at my phone, and it transformed itself before my eyes. It began to look like a cash register. No matter what happened on the other end of the line every time I made a call, I was making $10. I was able to associate touching the phone with making money. What could be more motivating than that? I could not have gotten there without tracking and reverse engineering my numbers. It was a game changer for me.

Over the years, I have observed that many salespeople resist tracking their activity. Here are a few reasons why.

- They feel they are solely doing it for management.
- They are uncomfortable with CRM.
- They don't see the benefit in doing it.
- They don't want to see how little activity they are doing.
- It takes time to do.

Here are ten reasons why you should track your activity:

1. **The only thing in life you can control is yourself**—your attitude and your effort. Therefore, that is the only thing you should track.

2. Your goal is to track your activity for yourself…not anyone else. **You are in competition with your own potential.** One way to see how you are doing is to track what you do.

3. **Tracking activity promotes more activity.** Objects in motion tend to stay in motion. Objects at rest tend to stay at rest. Activity typically generates more activity.

4. When you track your activities, **you will be living in reality** instead of rationalizing your behavior. High achievers make the choice to live in reality, because that is the starting point to developing the right prospecting mindset.

5. Tracking your activity every day will help you to **develop good habits**. Long after you can do anything about it, your habits will have created who you are.

6. **Use a system to track your activities**. The three most common ways are: Excel, CRM, a daily scorecard, or a combination thereof. Use what works best for you and use it every day. The easiest way to track your prospecting activities is while you are doing them.

7. Tracking your activity will enable you to determine how much you have completed toward your goal. This will show you what you need to do to stay on pace at any given moment, giving you **real-time feedback** on your where you stand in relation to achieving your goals.

8. **Understanding your conversion rates** is very important in helping you to reverse engineer your prospecting activities. For example, if you were able to see how many prospects you had to ask for a meeting in order to achieve your weekly goals, you would know how many asks you needed to make on a daily basis. You can also do what I did, which was to see how much money each prospecting attempt was worth.

9. Activity tracking will help you to get a true understanding of what is really happening in your prospecting activities. It will

also let you know **the precise activities that are driving opportunities into your pipeline.**

10. At the end of each day, week, and month, add up your numbers and analyze your efforts. **Make adjustments**, if necessary. Those adjustments are the fastest way to improve your skills and maximize your time.

The bottom line is that it doesn't matter how you track your activity. It only matters <u>that</u> you track your activity. You owe it to yourself to do so. What to do? Start tracking your prospecting activity today.

# PART III

# PROSPECTING TACTICS

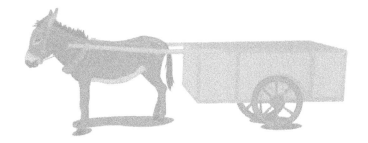

# CHAPTER 4

# LINKEDIN

# TIP 44

# Develop a daily LinkedIn routine.

As a prospecting tool, LinkedIn is not the be all, end all, but it is a resource that helps with a variety of prospecting activities. It is a tool that can help you to:

- Connect with clients and prospects.
- Gain market intelligence and conduct research.
- Post thought leadership and stay top of mind with your network.
- Source prospects that fit your ideal client profile.
- Ask your connections for introductions that fit your ideal client profile.

LinkedIn provides important information about your network—your 1st degree connections—giving you a way to connect with clients and prospects to **deepen relationships**. As you learn how to use the tool to fit your needs, incorporate a few best practices into your daily or weekly routine.

When I first got on LinkedIn, it was a black hole for me. I was reading, I was commenting, I was watching videos, but I was not really focused on any real prospecting activity on LinkedIn. So, I decided to create my own daily LinkedIn routine that allowed me to optimize the time I was spending on LinkedIn. I called it the Eight-Step Daily LinkedIn Routine, which means it was an eight-step process I followed from one to eight. I did it **every day** and made it a routine. The eight steps give you efficiency by having a **consistent process** to follow, and it gives you effectiveness of doing the most impactful activities.

So, I wrote it out and posted it above my computer. I follow it every day, each morning, while I drink a Dr. Pepper.

What to do? Develop a LinkedIn routine using the format on the next page.

# TIP 45

# What does a daily LinkedIn routine look like?

Here is an example of my eight-step daily LinkedIn Routine. This might help you to create your own daily LinkedIn routine.

1. Go to LinkedIn Home Page

    • Three likes or comments

2. Check My Network

    • Respond to pending invitations.

3. Go to Notifications

    • Birthdays, job changes, anniversaries, and promotions

4. Share Content

    • Post one video a week, four times per month.

5. Send Thank You Messages When Others Perform Actions

    • Invitations to connect, accepted my invitation, congratulated me, liked or commented on one of my video posts.

6. Send Connection Requests

    • Send ___ connection request/day.

7. Ask Connections to Meet

    • Ask ___ connection per day for a meeting.

8. Ask for Introductions

- Ask ___ connection per day for an introduction to a prospect.

What to do? After you create your daily LinkedIn routine, follow it every day.

# TIP 46

# Create templates for communicating on LinkedIn.

One way to be very efficient when going through your daily routine is to have customizable templates. The benefits to using templates are that they give you a starting point and are a shortcut, saving you time. Here are some examples of the ones I use.

1. They accept your invitation to connect:

   (Name) thanks for connecting with me. Talk soon.

2. They view your profile:

   (Name), I noticed you viewed my profile. We should connect soon.

3. They post a video or an article:

   Great post on (topic).

4. They like or comment on your post:

   Glad you enjoyed it (or) I always appreciate your insight on my posts.

5. They update their profile (e.g., post a new photo, new skills, etc.):

   That's an excellent photo!

6. They got a new job:

   Congratulations on the new job! Can't wait to catch up and hear more about it.

7. They have a work anniversary:

   Congratulations on your work anniversary. Nice job!

8. They have a birthday:

   Happy birthday! Hope you have a great day.

What to do? Use these examples to create your own template and use it for communicating on LinkedIn.

# TIP 47

# Set up a drip campaign on LinkedIn.

A drip campaign is a communication strategy that sends—drips—a pre-written set of messages to prospects over time. Simply put, it's sending prospects a series of messages over time to get them interested in you, what you do, and potentially working together. Here is an example of my LinkedIn six-step drip campaign.

| Message 1 | Ask to Connect | (Name), we've never met but I saw your profile on LinkedIn and wanted to reach out. I noticed we share a few connections in common, including (connection's name), who is a good friend and client of mine. We've helped (business outcome created). Maybe we can add value to you. Let's connect. |
| --- | --- | --- |
| Message 2 | Thanks for connecting | (Name) thanks for connecting. (Comment on something you have in common, something you are interested in learning more about them, or something that might be of help to them.) Looking forward to staying in touch. Thanks. |
| Message 3 | Direct to website | (Name) I hope business is going well for you. We're working with a variety of financial services firms and thought you would be interested in some of the things we're doing for them. You can check us out here: https://nextlevelsalesconsulting.com/home/industries/wealth-management/ Thanks, and talk soon. |
| Message 4 | Direct to YouTube channel | (Name) I'd like to keep you up to date with all of the video posts I'm doing on LinkedIn because they are all on my YouTube channel. Here is the link: https://www.youtube.com/channel/UCOmMsnTX8HcyCfMIwURf_4Q/playlists New videos are posted every week. Thanks. |
| Message 5 | Ask to Meet | (Name) Hope you're doing well. As you are probably aware by now, we specialize in working with financial services firms like yours, helping them to increase financial advisor productivity. Why don't we get together one day for fifteen minutes to meet each other? Here is my email stevej@tnlsc.com if you're interested so we can set something up. I hope to hear from you soon. |

| Message 6 | Follow-up | Hello (name), I've tried reaching out a few times but haven't heard back. I really believe we can add value to your situation based on our experience in working with wealth management firms. What is the main reason I haven't heard from you? I've added options to make it easier: |
|---|---|---|

1. Been busy but I am interested in meeting for fifteen minutes to find out more.
2. The timing isn't right, but I am interested in meeting for fifteen minutes now so that, when the need arises, we have a relationship with each other.
3. No need right now – but open to meeting later when the need arises.
4. Thanks, but not interested.

Just out of curiosity, is it 1, 2, 3, or 4?

What to do? Use this six-step example LinkedIn drip campaign to create your own.

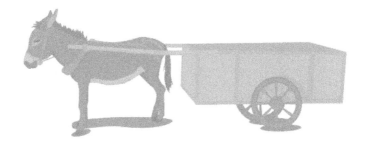

# CHAPTER 5

# RESEARCH DRIVEN
# OUTREACH

# TIP 48

# To script or not to script? That is the question. Here is the answer.

On my second day in sales, my manager gave me my first script, which was called the coffee talk. We practiced the coffee talk over and over until I felt confident with it. I still remember it today:

Hello, prospect, let's get together for a cup of coffee. We can learn about you, and you can learn about us. If there is a good fit, we can talk about possible steps, and if there isn't, we can shake hands and be friends. How does that sound? Would sometime in the morning or afternoon be better?

As I began to get ready for my first call blitz of the day, I was still pretty nervous, so I put the coffee talk script in front of me. I was also thinking about what I would do if I actually got a meeting, because I had never had a cup of coffee in my life.

In one of my first calls of the day, there was no gatekeeper and I got right through to the first prospect I ever talked to in my life. His name was Peter Dinerman. I panicked, looked at down my script, and the first words I said were, "Hello, prospect."

He started to laugh and asked me a few questions to make me feel more comfortable. I told him I was new, and he said, "You work for a great company. Come on down tomorrow morning. I am interested in learning more about the Dale Carnegie sales course."

What is interesting about my script, the coffee talk, is that I have never had a cup of coffee in my life and have asked over 150,000 prospects to get together for a cup of coffee. I much prefer soda pop. Particularly Dr. Pepper. My first script, the coffee talk, has never let me down. I have been using it throughout my career.

We have been very fortunate to work with a number of successful sales organizations, and it is surprising to me that so many salespeople are resistant to using a script. They say things like:

- I don't want to sound robotic.
- I don't want to sound salesy.
- I don't talk like that.

What they fail to understand is that they are already scripted! They say the same things over and over again, just like they wear the same clothes 80% of the time and eat the same food 80% of the time. Everyone has habits that are formed over time through repetition. The question is are they effective?

So, why should you use a script? Singers use lyrics. Sports teams run plays. Dancers do routines, and actors use scripts. They just practice them so many times that it becomes part of who they are. If you don't like the idea of using a script, think of it as **pre-memorized language**. Think of it as a **bridge to competency**. There are many benefits of using a script. Scripts:

- Are typically based on best practices of top performers.
- Give you a good starting point to work from.
- Give you something to practice.
- Can serve as a blueprint to refine and make your own.
- Build your confidence.
- Help you sound more natural when well-practiced.

Remember, anytime you see some of the most highly compensated people in our society perform—singers, dancers, actors, athletes—you know they are working from lyrics, routines, scripts, and plays.

What to do? After you do your research, customize your scripts to your target market and practice them so many times that they feel and sound natural for you.

# TIP 49

# Three things a gatekeeper wants to know and what you should do.

Over 80,000 gatekeepers in the greater Los Angeles area attended a rally at SoFi Stadium. The motivational speakers they had on hand to train, coach, and inspire the gatekeepers were Tony Robbins, Dwayne "The Rock" Johnson, and Arnold Schwarzenegger. The speakers spent a full day running these gatekeepers through live drills on how to screen calls.

Guess who you have to help **you** interact with these motivated gatekeepers? This guy. Steven Johnson, the guy who has made over 150,000 calls and interacted with gatekeepers on virtually every one of those calls.

As you painfully know, the gatekeeper is anyone who blocks you from contacting the decision maker: a receptionist, secretary, or an executive assistant. Depending on the level of the decision maker in the company you are calling, you could potentially come across all three.

From my experience, the three things a gatekeeper needs to know about you before putting your call through to the decision maker are:

1. Who are you?
2. What company are you with?
3. What is this regarding, about, in reference to, or are they expecting your call?

The person who asks questions is in control of the conversation; therefore, you want to identify yourself and the company you work for upfront to eliminate the two most common questions the gatekeeper will ask. It might sound something like this.

"Good morning, this is Steve Johnson with the Next Level for Bill Smith, please..." (Strategic pause.)

My voice tone is **firm and friendly** with the gatekeeper. Notice the use of the strategic pause after I say the word, please. The way I say the word "please" is matter of fact, as a statement not a question, indicating that I believe with every fiber of my being my call will get put through to the decision maker. That belief system alone will get you through to more decision makers.

In addition to my voice tone, notice that I am not saying any words that don't work like

- Is Bill Smith in?
- Is Bill Smith available?
- Can I speak with Bill Smith?

From my experience, if you ask these questions, you are shooting yourself in the foot and giving the gatekeeper the opportunity to say that Bill Smith is not in or, even if he is in, that he is not available. This strategy will improve your odds over time, because it is somewhat unconventional and gets the gatekeeper out of their rhythm, which is:

- Who are you?
- What company are you with?
- What is this regarding?

When they don't get the opportunity to ask these first two questions immediately because you answered them with your opening line, your chances increase ever so slightly of getting through to the decision maker. If the gatekeeper did not hear my name correctly the first time, they will often ask, "What was your name again?" What I do then is apologize because I was probably talking too fast in my introduction. I will slow down and restate my name like this.

"I'm sorry. This is Steve Johnson. Thank you." (Strategic pause)

What is different about this is the "thank you" and the use of another strategic pause. One more time, it goes like this.

"I'm sorry. This is Steve Johnson. Thank you." (Strategic pause)

The gatekeeper asked me for my name, and I told them the truth. It is Steve Johnson. The strategic pause after the thank you will increase your odds of getting through to the decision maker because it is an unanticipated approach. You say thank you in a way that comes across as a statement and sounds like you assume your call will be put through.

At this point, your call may be put through. However, the gatekeeper may have one more question to ask, which is: What is this regarding? We will cover how to answer that question in the next tip about four magic words to use with gatekeepers.

When you have made as many calls as I have and have been rejected as many times as I have, you become amazingly open-minded to what else is out there. When I initially tried out these strategies, they felt uncomfortable, but I found they actually worked better than what I was doing. I discovered I would rather **be uncomfortable doing things that worked rather than comfortable doing things that didn't work.**

What to do? Script out and practice your opening line. When you encounter a gatekeeper, state your name and the company you work for upfront in a tone that is firm and friendly, and assume your call will be put through.

# TIP 50

# Four magic words to use with gatekeepers.

When the gatekeeper asks something like, "What is this in reference to?" you will ask them for their help. Your four magic words are simply "**I need your help**." You will then use the same basic process that is used when speaking to a decision maker. You deliver your value proposition to the gatekeeper, so they know that you have a compelling reason for calling the decision maker. You then ask the gatekeeper questions designed to gather information that will enable you to find alternate ways to get through to the decision maker or to learn more about them.

Your entire goal is to win on the margins. Getting through to one extra decision maker per day is five a week, 20 per month and 240 by the end of the year. The reason why "I need your help" will help you do that is because people like to help other people. Asking for their help appeals to their nobler motives. Your opening line will sound something like this:

"Good morning. This is Steve Johnson with the Next Level for Bill Smith please."

After the opening line, you have eliminated the two questions the gatekeeper will ask which are: who are you? What company are you with? The next question they typically ask is something like:

"What is this in reference to?"

That is when you will use the four magic words. "I need your help." Then state your value proposition and ask for the decision maker. If they are not available, you will begin to ask the gatekeeper questions to gain more information. It might sound something like this.

"I need your help. We work with wealth management firms helping them to increase the first-year retention rate of new trainees. Is Bill Smith in right now?"

If the decision maker is not available, your goal is to ask questions to determine alternate ways to contact them that do not entail interacting with the gatekeeper. It might sound something like this.

"What is the best way to get in contact with Bill? Does he prefer email, cell phone, or does he have a direct dial extension?"

If you are unable to determine an alternate way to contact the decision maker, you can then ask:

"What is the best time to reach Bill?"

I have learned that quite often the best time to reach the decision maker is early, at lunch, or late in the day when the gatekeeper potentially is not there. I have also found that, when I contact a decision maker at these times, I develop credibility with them because I am hustling, just like them. They appreciate the work ethic.

Finally, I end every call by asking the gatekeeper for their name. I have found that by doing this I can establish rapport with the gatekeeper and, if I am politely persistent with my attempts to get through to the decision maker, it can increase my chances of getting access.

I close the call by thanking the gatekeeper for their help. Remember a little difference can make a big difference. Through asking the gatekeeper the four magic words, you will get through to more decision makers, set more meetings, and create more opportunities. Using "I need your help" will not get you through to every single decision maker every single time. But what it will do is improve your chances for success.

What to do? Take a yellow sticky note out right now and write "I need your help" on it and place it right above your phone.

# TIP 51

# Five ways to build rapport with gatekeepers.

**W**hen calling business owners, corporate executives, and working professionals, the reality is that you are going to encounter gatekeepers. There is no way around it. The gatekeeper plays a very important role, and one of your objectives is to build rapport with them. This is a long-term play, and you want to **form a friendly relationship with the gatekeeper.** Here are some best practices for building rapport with gatekeepers.

1.  **Be on a first name basis** with the gatekeeper. Learn their name, write it down, use it in conversation, log it in your notes for the decision maker.
2.  **Be respectful, polite, and friendly.** Use the words please and thank you. Never underestimate the influence that the gatekeeper has.
3.  **Be honest with the gatekeeper.** Don't be evasive or deceptive. You will sound more professional and worthy of being passed through to the decision maker.
4.  **Leverage the gatekeeper's knowledge.** Ask them for their help, advice, or information. For example,

    *   Ask if they handle the decision maker's schedule.
    *   Ask for the decision maker's email address, cell phone number, extension, or direct line.
    *   Ask if there is a better time to reach the decision maker or if you should leave a voicemail for them.
    *   Ask if there is another decision maker you should be speaking with.

5. **Change the game.** Sometimes the best strategy is to bypass the gatekeeper. This can be accomplished in a few ways.

- Try to meet the decision maker at an event.
- Send the decision maker an email.
- Send a handwritten note. This will get through for sure, as there are fewer and fewer salespeople doing this.
- Call early or late when the gatekeeper is potentially not there.
- Leverage social media to connect with the decision maker. One way to do this is by sending a LinkedIn InMail.

**The gatekeeper is not your enemy.** Their job is to screen out people that they think will waste the decision maker's time. The best way to approach the gatekeeper is simply to get the gatekeeper on your side. Seeing them as an immovable or impenetrable barrier will not help. Develop a friendly relationship with them using these best practices. Most importantly, treat them like you want to be treated.

What to do? Select one of these five ideas and try it out on your next call.

# TIP 52

# Have a voicemail strategy.

After making my fair share of outbound calls, I came to realize that no matter how good I was at making calls, how good my list was, or how well I stayed in my time block, the majority of my calls ended up in voicemail. I asked myself these questions about leaving a voicemail message.

- Will it be worth my time?
- Will it be a waste of my time?
- What will I say?
- Will my message generate a callback?

I realized the answers to those questions was…it depends. After trial and error and figuring out what worked and didn't work, I landed on a strategy that worked for me by bucketing my calls into three groups:

- Hot – hot opportunities were a referred prospect, a follow up to an introduction, or response to a request or demonstration of interest from the prospect.
- Warm – warm calls were the ones that I had done some research on the prospect.
- Cold – cold leads were those with no research, no introduction, and little information on the prospect.

On average, I did three sixty-minute call blitzes each day, the first two focused on hot and warm leads and the final one on cold leads. I averaged fifty outbound calls each day. I found I had a higher contact ratio with hot and warm leads than I did with cold leads. I also found I was spending one third of my time leaving voicemail. Also, when I left voicemail messages with hot and warm leads, I received a higher percentage of call backs than I did with cold leads.

Over time, I discovered that, within my sixty-minute time block with cold leads, I was spending about twenty minutes leaving messages – twenty to thirty seconds listening to each recorded message and that much time again for me to leave my message. When I realized that the callback ratio on my voicemails to cold leads was so low, I decided I would rather spend the twenty minutes that I was leaving voicemail messages making more calls.

I ultimately decided to call cold leads six times before leaving a voicemail message. I would call them six times on different days of the week and at different times of the day. If I still did not get in touch with them, I would then leave a voicemail on the sixth call.

What to do? I arrived at my voicemail strategy based on the best use of my time. You need to do the same. If you do decide to leave a voicemail, make sure that it is good.

# TIP 53

# If you're going to leave a voicemail, make it a good one.

Having had a career in sales and learning the best practices of top-performing salespeople from the companies we have worked with along the way, I have compiled a list of things to do to help **improve the callback ratio** from voicemails. Here are the fifteen best practices you should follow when you leave voicemails.

1. **Conduct research.** Through your research, you will be able to leave a personalized message to the prospect. The message could contain a compliment, the name of a common connection, or an idea you can share that is relevant to them.

2. **Use an attention-getter** on the front end of your voicemail. An attention-getter is like a headline in the news that draws the reader in and creates curiosity, so they click the link to learn more. The same thing happens when leaving a voicemail. You want to lead with an attention-getter first to create curiosity, so they are more inclined to listen to the rest of the message. This is especially true if the attention-getter is customized to the prospect based on something you uncovered in your research, or some common pain point you know is typical in their industry. This is typically the reverse of the typical voicemail – most salespeople state their name, their company, and the reason for the call first. Then comes the "attention-getter." When the attention-getter comes about fifteen seconds in, many times the prospect has already deleted the voicemail. For example,

   • (Prospect's name) My compliments on the article you posted on LinkedIn.

- (Prospect's name) I was on your website and noticed ____.
- (Prospect's name) I just got off the phone with a mutual friend of ours who had a lot of good things to say about you. This is Steve Johnson with The Next Level. The reason for the call is...

3. **Create and use scripts.** To save time and be more efficient with your voicemail you can create your voicemail scripts using a template. You will customize your scripts based on the information you learned about your prospect when you conducted your research. A voicemail template will help you customize your script and will generally follows this format:

   - Begin with prospect's name.
   - Attention-getter.
   - State your name, company, and reason for the call.
   - Request a specific call to action.
   - End with your contact information.

4. Use their name. Using their name personalizes the message, gets their attention, and may motivate them to listen to the rest of the voicemail.

5. **State the reason for your call.** This answers the question in the prospect's mind, "What's this call about?" This helps the prospect understand your offer and puts them in the position to decide if they are interested or not.

6. **Practice what you are going to say.** When you practice, you will get your message to sound exactly the way you want it to sound before you make the call.

7. **Leave the voicemail — don't hang up.** When you get to voicemail, one of two things will happen – you will either leave a voicemail or not. If you don't leave a message, the prospect will not be in a position to hear your offer. The downside to that is they do not have any motivation to call you back. If you do leave a message, and it piques their interest, they may decide to call you back.

8. **Be yourself** – show your personality. If you are making a lot of calls, you will be leaving a lot of voicemails. At some point you may start to sound robotic. Remember to make sure that

your personality shines through in your message on every call through your voice tone, inflection, and enthusiasm.

9. **Keep it brief.** Keep it brief. Keep it brief. Maximum fifteen to thirty seconds.

10. **Speak slowly.** There is a natural tendency when leaving a voicemail to talk fast. In reality, you want to say fewer words and speak slowly. When you do this, you will sound more self-confident and professional.

11. **Mention you work with similar prospects.** A good strategy when leaving voicemail is to mention that you work with clients that are similar to them and have added value to those prospects by helping them achieve some of the outcomes they were looking for. Prospects like to know that you are knowledgeable and credible in working with people who are similar to themselves.

12. **Request a specific call to action.** Give the prospect something to do—give you a call, send you a text, or send you an email. Whatever you want them to do, ask them to do it. Anything can happen.

13. **Mention that you will follow up.** You can use your voicemail message as a heads-up to let them know that you will be attempting to contact them through LinkedIn or via email.

14. **End with your contact information.** You will state your name, phone number, and/or email, two times.

15. **Don't forget the goal of the message.** The goal is not to sell. The goal is to generate a callback and/or warm up your next touchpoint with the prospect.

What to do? Review these best practices periodically and implement them when leaving voicemails.

# TIP 54

# Use an effective voicemail drip campaign.

arlier in this book, we introduced the notion of having a LinkedIn drip
campaign. You can also have a voicemail drip campaign, which is a
communication strategy for leaving prospects a series of messages over
time to generate a callback. Some research indicates that, every time you
leave a voicemail, you increase the chance of getting a callback. Therefore,
you will want to do this in an **intentional and purposeful manner**.

Previously, we discussed creating and using voicemail templates for
your messages. Using those templates will save you time when you execute
voicemail drip campaigns.

Here are some ideas for an effective voicemail drip campaign:

1.  **Don't leave only one voicemail.**

    •   You want to assume that they didn't listen to it.

2.  **Determine your strategy.**

    •   How many messages will you leave?
    •   What is the frequency, timing, etc.?
    •   What are the messages?

3.  **On subsequent voicemails, vary your messages.** Have multiple scripts.

    •   Continue to do research.
    •   Vary your messages by using a new attention-getter that
        is timely, relevant, and might pique the prospect's interest
        enough to call you back.

- Here are some example attention-getters for a voicemail drip campaign:
    - (Prospect's name) I noticed your competitor is doing ____.
    - (Prospect's name) I saw your company recently ____.
    - (Prospect's name) Are you experiencing (challenges) with your business?
    - (Prospect's name) Have you considered (solution) to improve your (business outcome)?

4. Remember that **each voicemail is another touch** that may lead to a callback.
5. **Keep notes** on which voicemail message you leave each time, so you know how many attempts you have made and what was said.

What to do? If you find yourself leaving a lot of voicemail messages, you may want to consider creating a drip campaign that you can do over time, with different messages, that will generate callbacks.

# TIP 55

# What not to say when you get a prospect on the phone.

L et's assume the gatekeeper has put your call through and you have the decision maker on the line. **The first five seconds can make or break you.** You don't want to use words, phrases, or questions that create resistance instead of interest in those first five seconds. I feel particularly qualified to discuss this topic based on the number of mistakes I have made when calling prospects. I have arrived at these conclusions after studying, practicing, and making adjustments based on what worked and didn't work.

So, before we talk about what to avoid saying, let me say a few things up front:

- Some of the things I am going to tell you to avoid saying may work at times, but not over the long haul. They may work based on personality or delivery style, but most people would fail using them consistently.
- These suggestions are meant to help you lower the probability that you are going to create resistance.
- Nothing works all the time. These suggestions are meant to increase your probability of success.

You may react to some of the things I point out by saying to yourself that you say these things all the time. I get it. I have made every mistake in the book. From the laboratory of human experience, in my opinion, here is what **NOT** to say:

1. I know you're busy. I'm sorry for interrupting.

   - You're always an interruption. Don't apologize for your doing your job, which is prospecting.

2.  I'm not trying to sell you anything.

    - Of course, the prospect knows that is the purpose of your call. They know why you are calling, and this statement adds no value and may actually create resistance.

3.  You and I have never spoken before.

    - Come on, you both know that you have never spoken to each other before. This statement is useless.

4.  I just wanted to...

    - Reach out to you.
    - Touch base with you.
    - Ask you a few questions.
    - Check in with you.

      Get rid of the word "just." It sounds weak and diminishes everything that follows it.

5.  Is now a good time?

      If you were a prospect and someone that you didn't know called you and asked if now was a good time, your typical reaction would be to say, "No, make it quick," or "What are you selling?"

      If it is in fact a bad time for prospects, let them tell you. Don't give them an out right away.

Now that you know five things to avoid saying when you get the prospect on the line, what are you going to do differently on your prospecting calls?

What to do? Think of the adjustments you need to make and put them into action.

# TIP 56

# What to say when you get a prospect on the phone.

O nce the gatekeeper has put your call through to the decision maker, you want to create interest and engagement in the first few seconds. The first thing you want to do is say something that demonstrates that you did your research before making the call. Second, you will want to clearly state the purpose of your call and deliver your value proposition. Then you will begin to ask questions based on the prospect's situation.

Let me give you some examples for each step:

First, you will **lead with your research**. This differentiates you by showing that you are not a typical cold caller. It personalizes your call and helps you develop credibility with the prospect.

For example, to help generate interest and engagement with the prospect, you may say something like:

- My compliments on the article you posted on LinkedIn.
- I was on your website and noticed your firm's insights on the market.
- I was speaking with Adriana Johnson the other day, and she mentioned that you were getting ready to revamp your new financial advisor training program.

Next, you will transition into **the purpose of the call** by saying, "The reason for the call is…" Then **deliver your value proposition**. For example,

- The reason for the call is that we specialize in working with wealth management firms, helping them to improve financial advisor productivity.

- The reason for the call is, from my research, it looks like you may be experiencing growth in your call centers.

Finally, you will transition into discovery by asking a question. Here is an example what this might sound like:

"Hello, Keith, I just read an article on Advisor Hub from your CEO about how your company is focusing on recruiting this year, which prompted me to reach out. The reason for the call is that we have worked with a number of financial services firms helping them to train and coach their managers to become better recruiters. What are you looking to accomplish with your recruiting efforts this year?"

In summary, in the first ten seconds of a call with a prospect, mention your research, state the reason for the call, deliver your value proposition, and ask a question. In doing these things, you are communicating to the prospect that you are not a typical cold caller. You did your research, which helps build credibility. You clearly stated your purpose for the call, which is your potential value-add to their situation. Finally, you asked a question, which demonstrates your interest in learning more about them.

Now that you know what to say when you get a prospect on the phone, what are you going to do differently on your prospecting calls?

What to do? Think of the adjustments you want to make when you get a prospect on the phone and put them into action.

# TIP 57

# Six magic words to use to set a meeting.

Through experience, I have learned that an important metric to track in sales is the number of meetings you set with prospects. Typically, the more meetings you set, the better you will get at setting meetings. How you conduct those meetings will have a big impact on your success as well, but the most important piece of the puzzle is setting the meeting in the first place. What you say to set up a meeting can make a big difference.

So, I am going to walk you through the six magic words to use when asking a prospect for a meeting. The first two words are "**get together**." These work well because they sound far less formal and more relaxed than the word "appointment." Words three and four are "**add value**." Adding value is what everyone is talking about and seems to be how we are all measured. The last two words are "**good fit**." These two words are disarming and communicate to the prospect that you are just as interested in seeing if they are a good fit for you as you are in seeing if you are a good fit for them.

There are two types of cologne you can wear in sales, passion and desperation, and you can smell desperation a mile away. "**Good fit**" implies that you are not desperate.

So, let's say you have had a meaningful conversation with a prospect, and you are ready to ask for the meeting. It might go something like this.

"(Prospect's name,) let's **get together** for a cup of coffee. We can learn more about you and let you know how we work with our clients. We may be able to **add value** to your situation because we work with other wealth management firms that are similar to yours. If there is a **good fit**, we can discuss possible next steps. How do you look next week?"

What to do? Get a pad of paper out and write down the six magic words to use to ask a prospect for a meeting. Practice it and then give it a try.

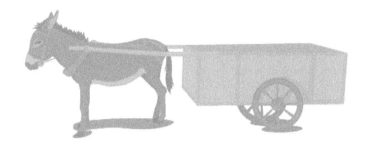

# CHAPTER 6

# NETWORKING AT EVENTS

# TIP 58

# Where to network? Birds of a feather flock together.

**B**irds of a feather flock together. People tend to associate with others who share **similar interests**. To optimize your networking effectiveness, you must do one thing well. Go where your clients and prospects are likely to be. For ideas on where to go, **ask your clients** where they go and ask them if you can go there with them. Once you identify those places where your clients and prospects go, **attend consistently** to generate contacts, build relationships, and set meetings. Here is what has worked for me.

I have had success at industry associations. We sponsor events, and I can see who is coming to the event, target who I want to meet, and see what's going on in the industry. Most importantly, I get face time with people who are in my target market that fit my ideal client profile. A side benefit is that I am able to see what my competitors are doing, and it helps me to know how to differentiate myself from them.

Trade shows are another opportunity where we have had success. Because we have a booth, we are able to source the list of attendees in advance. We can send an email to the prospects that we want to meet and invite them to our booth to get a free book. A few other benefits of trade shows are that you can network, attend breakouts that you are interested in, and be a presenter.

There are countless number of places to go to network. A few best practices are to go consistently, build relationships, get into a leadership role, and be a presenter.

What to do? A good place to start is to ask your ten best clients where they go. See if you can go there with them. Remember, birds of a feather flock together.

# TIP 59

# Do pre-work before you network.

There is a one-letter difference between networking and not working. The more preparation you do before you go to a networking event, the more you will ensure that, when you are networking, your net is working. Here are four tips for preparing for a networking event.

1.  **Set goals for the event.** Before I go to any event, I begin with the end in mind through setting my goals for attending. I ask myself: Why am I attending this event? What am I trying to achieve? Who do I want to meet? Goal setting will help you to maximize your time at the event and measure your success.

2.  If possible, **research attendees** who will be attending the event. If I am able to find the names of the hosts, attendees, or presenters of the event, I will go to LinkedIn Sales Navigator, Google, Facebook to learn more about them. When I'm at the event, this information helps me to create a connection. Researching attendees prior to the event will help you to establish common ground easily at the event.

3.  **Prepare a relevant compliment or conversation starter** from your research. When I am doing my research on someone, I am looking for things that stand out, such as career progression, their current role, or thought leadership they have either posted or written. Prepare relevant conversation starters or compliments from your research.

4.  **Be prepared to answer the question of what you do for work.** I am going to go into any event with my elevator pitch ready, especially if I am attending events with prospects who are right in my wheelhouse. When someone asks me what I do, I have my elevator pitch ready.

What to do? Remember there is a one-letter difference between networking and not working. Doing pre-work before you network will help you to make your net is working when you are networking.

# TIP 60

# Make sure that, when you are networking, your net is working.

D epending on the goals for networking, most people are going to events to make new contacts, build relationships and generate business from their efforts. In today's digital world, there is nothing more valuable than face-to-face interaction. Because of that, you want to make sure that you are in a position to **maximize your time** when you are at a networking event, thus helping you to achieve your goals. I could go on for several pages about all of the things to do to get the most out of each event, but I will share five tips.

1. **Show up early.** When I get to a networking event early, I can strategize what I want to do to achieve my goals for attending the event. I can see who is coming in and where they are sitting. I can meet the host and presenter. Arriving early can help you work the room more strategically and help you achieve your goal for the event.

2. Have a way to **remember names**. When I meet someone new, I create an association for their name. I use some mechanism to remember the name, a rhyme, thinking about someone I know with the same name, or I link the name to an image that can trigger my memory. Once I learn someone's name, I try to use it in conversation. When you meet someone new, find a way to remember their name and then use their name in conversation.

3. **Target who you want to meet** prior to the event. Before the event, I have a target list of who I want to meet based on my research. At the event, I approach those people and tell them I was looking forward to meeting them there. Don't be shy at a networking event – approach the people you are there to meet.

4. **Exchange cards/contact information and make notes**. After I have had a conversation with someone and we have exchanged contact information, I write notes on the back of their card or document the notes on my phone about what we discussed as soon as possible. I give out my business cards from one pocket and put the business cards I get in the other pocket. After you have a meaningful conversation and exchanged contact information, take notes in a manner that works best for you.

5. **Ask them to connect on LinkedIn.** Once I have their contact information, I send them a connection request on LinkedIn while I am still at the event. My message to them on LinkedIn is something like this, "Great to meet you. Let's continue the conversation. How do you look for coffee next week?" LinkedIn is built for connecting with people while you are still at the event. It is a great way to strike while the iron is hot.

What to do? Select one of these five tips to use at your next networking event to make sure that when you are networking your net is working.

# TIP 61

# Master the art of grinning and gripping when networking.

A t the Next Level, we train about 5,000 salespeople per year; and, when we are working on networking skills and start to talk about the handshake, the room starts buzzing. Why is that? Because people remember bad handshakes, and your handshake is typically an element of the first impression you give. A bad first impression is sometimes hard to come back from. So, here are five tips on how to **make a good first impression** at an event with your handshake.

1. **Be prepared to shake hands**. When I am at events, I try to keep my right hand free by holding my cell phone in my left hand. If I have a drink, I try to set it down to keep my right hand free.
2. **Give the other person the gift of your full attention** when shaking their hand. I look them in the eye and smile when shaking their hand. If I am sitting down and we get introduced, I stand up to shake their hand.
3. **Shake their hand the right way.** The ideal handshake is web to web. I keep the notion of web-to-web in mind when I am shaking someone's hand. I try to have a firm and friendly grip, shake two to three times, and then let go.
4. **Timing matters** when shaking hands. I try to shake hands when I arrive, when I leave, or when I meet someone new. I try to avoid offering to shake someone's hand if they are talking to someone else.
5. **Practice your handshake** and get feedback, especially before you go to a networking event. It will make a difference. When my son Matthew got accepted into the University of Notre Dame, they held an admitted student day in Brentwood with the big brass at a local level. Before he left for the event, we prac-

ticed his handshake ten times. "Hello, it is nice to meet you. I am Matthew Johnson from Loyola High School." It must have worked. He graduated from Notre Dame. "Go Irish!!!"

Now that we have given you five tips on how to make a good first impression at an event with your handshake, here are some types of handshakes you want to avoid.

- The Dead Fish – This is a limp, lifeless handshake that does not inspire a lot of confidence or make a good first impression.
- The Vice Grip – This is when the grip is not web to web, and you grip their fingers from the knuckles down.
- The Politician – This is when the one-handed handshake hand turns into two hands and then it creeps up their wrist, arm, and up to the shoulder.
- The Terminator – This is a variation of the vice grip, its web to web, but the tilt of the wrist rolls over and then down.
- The Barnacle – This is after there are two to three shakes and you don't let go.
- The Queen of England –This is where you pinch their hand between your thumb and fingers.
- The Sweaty Palmer – This happens if you have been holding a cold drink in your right hand and the condensation from the glass makes your hand wet.

For your own benefit, you may want to try to avoid shaking anyone's hand at a networking event with these handshakes. There are also times at a networking event where you are shaking hands with someone you just met and, for whatever reason, you just did not get it right. It is okay to ask for a handshake redo to get it right. This solidifies a positive first impression.

What to do? If you want to master the art of grinning and gripping when you are networking, get the ideal handshake down and practice it to make sure you're doing it the right way.

# TIP 62

# Develop a way to remember names.

I remember one summer in August when I went to Tiffany and Company in Beverly Hills. I was with my two kids Matthew and Anna after a day at the beach. I wanted to look into getting my wife Elisa a pendant for her birthday which was in October. The store was the one in "Pretty Woman," right across the street from the Beverly Wilshire on Rodeo Drive. I was in shorts and a T-shirt, not really looking like the ideal client. I got some help, explained that I was not going to buy anything at the moment but would come back and get it closer to my wife's birthday.

Two months later, I went back to Tiffany and Company in Beverly Hills and the clerk said, "Hello, Mr. Johnson."

I thought to myself, *There is no way that I am **not** going to get that pendant now. She remembered my name.*

She had made an effort to remember my name, which demonstrated to me that she cared. She made a great impression on me, and I wanted to give her my business.

Dale Carnegie said it best when he said, "Remember that a person's name is, to that person, the sweetest and most important sound in any language." When networking, you will be meeting a lot of new people, and you want to make an effort to remember their names. So here are four tips that can help you remember names.

Tip one is to **focus on them.** I focus 100% of my attention on the person I am meeting and listen to their name. If I did not hear it clearly, I ask them for their name again, one more time.

Tip two is to **repeat their name**. I repeat their name in conversation, beyond just the initial introduction. I try to use their name in the conversation, if possible. Even if it is only at the end of the conversation, I like to say, "It was nice to meet you, (name.)" That is better than nothing and helps me to remember their name.

Tip three is to **create an association for their name**. I work out at 5:00 in the morning at the Bay Club in Manhattan Beach. I see the same people all the time. I have made a commitment to remember their names, because I see them three to four times a week. There is Dan the man, cup of Joe, Marky Mark, Frank the Tank, I like Mike, George of the Jungle, Peg-leg Craig. You get the idea.

Tip four is to **ask them their name if you can't remember it**. When I forget someone's name, I simply ask them for their name again. I found that this is safer to ask them for their name again, rather than not being able to remember it and being embarrassed.

I have met countless people who have said they are not good at remembering names. It seems like a lot of work to get good at it, but the work is worth the effort. You know the good feeling you get when someone remembers your name? They feel the same way when you remember theirs.

What to do? When you meet somebody, give them 100% of your attention, use their name in conversation, create a way to remember their name, and if you forget their name, remember that it's okay to ask.

# TIP 63

# Ask a question to start a conversation at a networking event.

One of my favorite Dale Carnegie quotes is, **"Be interested rather than interesting."** One way to demonstrate your interest in others at networking events is to have a genuine sense of curiosity and ask the right questions. That is why networking is easy. There is no pressure. Many people like to talk about themselves and their interests. As they do, they develop an affinity and a liking for you.

Let's assume you have done things right, you have introduced yourself, you have shaken hands, etc. Now it's time to start the conversation. One way to start a conversation is to ask a question.

Here are four questions I use as conversation starters:

1.  What brought you to the event?

    I ask this question to understand why they are there. When I understand why they are there, it helps me to think about other questions I can ask. For example, if I ask them what brought them to the event, and they say it's their first time there, I will ask questions about that.

2.  What do you do for work?

    One of the main reasons why I ask somebody what they do for work is that it enables me to think about other questions I can ask them about their career, job, or role. For example, if I ask them what they do for work and they say they're the head of the private bank at company XYZ, I might say, "What are some of the biggest priorities you are trying to accomplish with your sales team this year?"

3. How do you like the venue?

One of the reasons why I ask this question is because it's an easy question to ask. It's not business related, job specific, or too personal and can generate a conversation quickly. You can also mention other venues you have been to which compare well to the one you are in. Oftentimes, as they discuss the venue, they will compare it to other venues they have been to as well.

4. What did you like about the speaker today?

I like to ask this question to start a conversation because everybody interprets a speaker differently. Asking people for their perspective is a warm approach to beginning a conversation. It also can help establish common ground, if you both feel the same way about what the speaker had to say.

Remember to be interested instead of interesting. A great way to get a conversation going is to ask a question. Conversation starters will help you to establish common ground, build rapport, and create a connection.

What to do? At the next event you attend. Ask a question to get a conversation going.

# TIP 64

# Have a conversation exit plan.

I t can be an awkward moment for you at a networking event—you want to move on but aren't sure how to make a graceful exit. Having attended countless events and finding myself in that situation many times, I find it helpful to **anticipate** when I want to end the conversation, **give a reason** for moving on, and then say something to **make the other person feel good** about the time we spent together.

Here are five ways to end the conversation at an event.

1. **Simply end the conversation respectfully.**

   Sometimes, even when you've met someone interesting, the time comes when you're ready to move on. You might say something like, "(Name), it was nice to meet you. I'm going to take a look at some of the other exhibits here, but if I don't run into you later, I hope to see you at another event soon."

2. **Offer to connect later.**

   If you meet someone who is a valuable contact, make sure to exchange information before you leave. For example: "(Name), I have to leave, but I really enjoyed meeting you. Is it possible to get your contact information so we can schedule a time for us to finish our conversation?"

3. **Plan a follow-up date.**

   If you think that you'll run into this contact at another upcoming event, why not plan to attend together? This helps you build a relationship with a good connection and can help you feel more comfortable at the next event. For example: "It was great to meet you today. Are you planning to go to the association's meeting next month? If so, maybe we could go together."

4. **Get advice and move on.**

A new contact can be a valuable resource, but that doesn't mean you need to stay with them the entire time. When it's time to part ways, be honest that you'd like to follow up at a later date, and then say a polite goodbye. For example: "(Name), I'm a new member at the Chamber of Commerce, and you have been a member here for quite some time. I would love to get your advice on how I can best get involved with the chamber. I want to talk to a few others here tonight, but can we plan to connect next week?"

5. **Simply end the conversation and move on.**

Sometimes, you just want to move on because you would like to meet more people. For example: "(Name), it's been great to meet you. I want to move on because I promised myself I want to meet at least five new people tonight." This strategy is typically effective to use at networking events that are designed for the sole purpose of helping attendees meet other professionals.

6. **Pull in another person.**

Another option is to simply pull in a third person and invite them to join in the conversation, especially if I know the third person has some common ground with the person I'm talking to.

What to do? If attending networking events is important to you, master the skill of gracefully exiting conversations.

# TIP 65

# Maximize your networking efforts through follow up.

I have been to my fair share of networking events, and I have made a ton of mistakes. I have learned that what I do at the event is important, but what I do after the event is even more important. When I don't follow up or don't follow up in a timely manner, I am not maximizing the opportunities that I generated at the event. Here are five tips on how to follow up after a networking event.

Tip one is that **speed matters**. Faster is better. There is a recency effect that wears off after you meet somebody at a networking event. Think of the law of diminishing returns. Your probability of success will be greatest the sooner you follow up. The longer you take to follow up, the lower your probability of success. Which leads to tip number two.

Tip two is to **block time on your calendar** for follow up at the same time you schedule the event. When I schedule a networking event in my calendar, I schedule time to follow up the day after the event. For example, if I have an event on my calendar on Thursday night, I will block time on Friday to do my follow up from the event.

Tip three is to **prioritize your follow-up**. What I do is I take all the business cards I collected at the event, I look at my notes on the back, and then I prioritize them in order of importance. Prioritize your follow up because every contact you make at a networking event is not equal. You will follow up with everybody, but you will follow up on your top priorities first.

Tip four is to **research the contacts** you made to personalize your follow up. Beyond the conversations I had at the event and the notes I took, I will look them up on Google, Twitter, Facebook, and their company website. If I didn't connect with them on LinkedIn at the event, I attempt to connect with them within twenty-four hours of the event. Do your research to help with the personalization of your follow up.

Tip five is to **customize your follow-up** based on the conversation you had at the event, particularly if they expressed interest in what you do. I include a one-pager that overviews our capabilities that I feel might be relevant to them. I sometimes send information or an article I feel might be of interest to them based on our conversation. I end the email with a call to action, such as a request to meet.

What to do? Select one or more of these five tips to use to follow up after your next networking event.

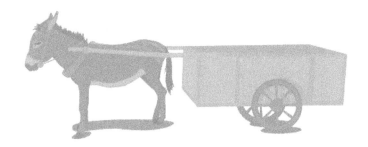

# CHAPTER 7

# PROSPECTING IN SOCIAL SITUATIONS

# TIP 66

# How to mix business with pleasure in a social setting.

Many salespeople would categorize prospecting in a social setting as mixing business with pleasure. The reason for this is that many of the social situations they find themselves in are with people who could be a good prospect for what they do. The last thing you want is to be the person in your circle of influence who everyone runs away from. Your fear is that, if you introduce business in these settings, people will run away from you. How many times have you been in a social situation and thought something like this?

- I'd love to talk business with Emma Jean, but if I do, I am worried that I might jeopardize our friendship.
- Emma Jean would be a great client, and I would love to tell her what I do, but I don't want her to think I'm pushy and avoid me at our kid's events.
- I don't know how Emma Jean would feel about me approaching her here.

Recognize that **there is a time and a place for everything**. The opportunity to discuss business with people you know socially has four key elements:

1. The equity you have built in the relationship.
2. How well you know the person.
3. Timing.
4. How you bring up the subject.

It might sound something like this. "(Name), I was thinking about you the other day. You and I have never talked business before. How about we get together for breakfast or lunch and explore some ideas I have. Is this something you'd be interested in doing?"

If the prospect is receptive, you would simply ask for a meeting by saying, "Great, what works for you?" If they are not interested, you don't want to fold up like a lawn chair. You will want to respond in a way that doesn't make them feel uncomfortable and leaves the door open for future conversations. It might sound like this. "No problem, (name). It was something I was thinking about that made sense to me, and I just wanted to see if you had any interest. If I can be a sounding board or a resource for you or anybody you know in the future, please let me know." Then go back to the social conversation.

Even though they were not interested, you accomplished two things.

1. **You got the offer out rather than doing nothing.** You did not make any assumptions about whether or not they were interested and let them make their own decision.
2. **You planted a seed for the future.** You offered yourself as a resource, and they may begin to view you in a different light than they have in the past. The bottom line is that anything can happen once you get the offer out. What have you got to lose?

What to do? In the next social situation that you are in, if the timing is right, get your offer out.

# CHAPTER 8

# ASKING FOR REFERRALS & INTRODUCTIONS

# TIP 67

# What is the best way to ask for referrals? Ask for advice.

think that most salespeople would agree that the fastest, best, and most sustainable way to build your business is by asking for referrals. Yet, having surveyed 5,000 of our clients on why they were not asking for referrals on a consistent basis, two-thirds of them said they haven't gotten into the **habit** of doing it, and the other third of them said they were **concerned** they would sound salesy, pushy, or desperate.

So, if you are overly concerned about how your clients will perceive you when you ask them for a referral, you don't need to worry about that anymore. You will never have to ask them for a referral. All you need to do is ask them for their advice.

So, why is this strategy so effective? Here is what I have learned. Many people like to be asked for advice, and many people like to give advice because it makes them **feel good** about themselves.

When I get asked for advice, I take it as a **compliment**. I develop a greater affinity and a liking for that person. When I give them my advice, I become more invested in their success and want to be kept in the loop on how they carried out the advice I gave them.

Building your business through referrals is a way to grow your business with the highest degree of velocity, especially if you are duplicating your best clients. There is a high degree of probability, due to **the law of similarity**, that your clients affiliate and assimilate with other people who are similar to themselves.

It might sound something like this:

"(Name), thank you for your business. Do you have a few minutes to give me some advice? I would like to build my business with people that are similar to you. What advice would you give me on how to meet more people like you?

- Where do they get together?
- What clubs, groups, or associations do you belong to?
- Besides you, who are the three or four most successful people in your network?"

I have been fortunate in my life to have great clients and have asked many of them for their advice. What I have found is that one of five things typically happens:

1. They **coach** me on how to meet more people like themselves.
2. They **invite** me to come with them to an event to introduce me to their network.
3. They **ask** me to speak at an event.
4. They **arrange** an introduction.
5. They **give** me a name.

What to do? Ask five of your best clients for advice on how you can meet more people that are just like them.

# TIP 68

# Make asking for referrals a habit.

Y ou conduct meetings with prospects and clients all the time. A good best practice to make sure you optimize the time spent in a meeting is to have a clearly defined **meeting agenda.** That agenda will include all the high-level topics you want to make sure you cover in the meeting. I typically use an agenda in my discovery, recommendation, and review meetings.

I have found a best practice is to put a bullet point as the last agenda item that simply says "Referral." As the meeting is wrapping up, I look down at my agenda and see "Referral" as the last item, which reminds me to ask. If you consistently put **"Referral"** as the last agenda item for every meeting, the activity of doing that will help you form the habit of asking for referrals.

Let's assume you are finishing a review meeting with a client, and it has gone well. You glance down at your agenda and the last bullet point is "Referral." The ask might sound something like this:

1. (Name), thanks for getting together today. We really appreciate you as a client. How do you feel about what we discussed today?
2. Is there anything else we could be doing better?
3. Great. Thanks for your feedback. As one of our clients, you have experienced the benefits of our approach and process. As you are probably aware, I work with the head of sales in organizations that are in a growth mode, have more than 500 salespeople, are willing to invest in those people, and are open to working with somebody from the outside. Does anybody come to mind? (Client responds with a name.)
4. Tell me a little bit about (name).
5. What is the best way to arrange an introduction to (name)?

What to do? As you prepare for your next meeting, put "Referral" as the last bullet point on your agenda to remind yourself to ask for a referral. Start building the habit.

# TIP 69

# Best approach to take when contacting a referral.

**W**hen a client gives you a name or offers to make a referral, it makes sense to learn more and to **prepare** before you attempt to make contact. You never get a second chance to make a good first impression. The last thing you want to do is be unprepared.

Here are five steps you can take before contacting a referral.

1. **Gather information from the client who arranged the referral.** Things like professional status, interests and hobbies, and other insights on their life can help you establish common ground.

2. **Ask the client for a warm handoff.** Ask them to introduce you to the referral or to make the referral aware that you will be contacting them. When you have been introduced to a referral through a mutual connection, they are more inclined to answer your call, return your call, or reply to your email. Of the five steps, this is the step that most often gets left out, and it's the step that makes the biggest difference. The warm handoff sets you up for success.

3. **Research the referral.** Go to LinkedIn and Google to learn more about them.

4. **Review social media sites.** Sites such as Facebook, Twitter, and Instagram can give you a window into who they are.

5. **Go to their company website** to learn what their company does and potentially gain insight into the prospect's role in the organization.

Once you have done your due diligence, it's time to make the call or send an introductory email. Either way, you will start by introducing yourself and the client who referred you to them. You will then state the purpose of the outreach and your value proposition. You will end by asking for a meeting. The call might sound something like this:

> "Good morning, (name). This is Steve Johnson with The Next Level. I just got off the phone with a mutual friend of ours, Elaine Jordan. She had a lot of good things to say about you. Are you curious about what she said?" (Mention any insights gained from the referral source to build rapport and establish common ground.)

> "The reason for the call is that we help wealth management firms improve advisor productivity so they can gain more market share. Elaine thought it would make sense for us to meet. How do you look next week for a cup of coffee?"

If you don't want to lead with a call, you can send a version of this in an email then follow up with a call.

What to do? When a client gives you a referral, do your research before reaching out. Be prepared. Use your research to attempt to build rapport and establish common ground.

# TIP 70

# Asking for an introduction versus a referral. What's the difference?

In addition to asking for referrals, I also ask clients or other centers of influence (COIs) to arrange introductions. For our purposes, I will refer to these sources as COIs. The difference between asking for referrals and introductions is that, when asking a COI for a **referral**, I describe my ideal client to them and then **ask them to think of someone** who might be a good fit for what I do. When asking a COI for an **introduction, I already have the name of a specific prospect** I know the COI knows.

In order to ask for introductions, I source names of specific prospects I would like a COI to introduce me to. Just like building my list of prospects to contact without an introduction, this is an ongoing process. It takes some time to source names of quality prospects. There are many ways to build a list of people who you would like to be introduced to. I'm just going to use a very common one, which is LinkedIn.

There are two ways I use LinkedIn to source the names of prospects that I would like to be introduced to through my connections:

1. I go to my connections profile and look at their 2nd degree connections. I look for prospects who are in my target market that I think might be a good fit for what I do.
2. I look for prospects who I would like to be introduced to and see if they are connected to any of my connections.

I use these two methods to build my list of COIs that I am connected to on LinkedIn that are also connected to the prospects I would like to get introduced to.

There is a difference between asking for referrals and asking for introductions. It is good to note the difference between the two. When asking for a referral, you are asking the COI to think of names for you.

When you ask for an introduction, you give them a name and ask them to introduce you.

What to do? Begin building a list of prospects you would like to be introduced to as well as the COIs who can make introductions for you.

# TIP 71

# How to ask for an introduction.

Once I have identified a prospect I would like to be introduced to, I prefer to make a phone call to ask for an introduction as opposed to using LinkedIn or through email. It doesn't mean you can't do it either of those ways. It is just that I prefer the personal approach with my COIs through a conversation. Here are three examples I use:

Example 1:

(Name), I noticed you are connected to ___. How well do you know her?

Do you think she would be a **good fit** for what I do?

I would really appreciate an introduction to ___. What would be the best way for you to introduce me socially?

Example 2:

(Name), I saw you were connected to a couple people on LinkedIn who look like the type of people we work with. I noticed ___. How well do you know him?

Do you think he is someone who might be a good fit for what we do?

What would be the best way for you to introduce me to him?

Example 3:

(Name), I was going to reach out to ___, and I noticed you were connected to her on LinkedIn. How well do you know her?

Do you think she would be a good fit for what we do?

I would like your advice on the best way for me to be introduced to ___?

In summary, once I have the names of my COI and prospects I want to be introduced to, I determine the approach I will take on the call. One key factor I'm looking to determine before I ask for the introduction is whether or not the prospect would be a good fit for what I do. Then I make the call and use the talking points that are best suited to the situation.

What to do? Prepare your approach and talking points prior to making the call to ask for an introduction.

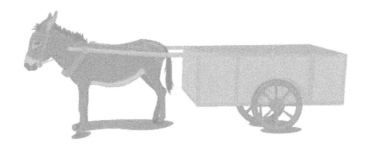

# CHAPTER 9

# EMAIL & TEXTING

# TIP 72

# Send emails that will get delivered, opened, and read.

One of the things we mentioned earlier in the book is that **the best prospecting approach is a balanced prospecting approach using multiple modalities of communication**. Email is a valuable part of that approach. People may not pick up your call or connect with you on LinkedIn, but they may respond to your email if you send a good one. Email is a very efficient way to prospect. You can write it at a time that works best for you, and the person you send it to can read it whenever they want.

The most important thing is that you want your email to get through. To increase the chances of that happening, here are some things to avoid:

- Sending batched emails. Batched emails are easily blocked, sent to a spam folder, or bounced back.
- Sending hyperlinks or attachments. Many firewalls are set to identify and block that type of content.
- Words that look and feel like spam in the subject line. The spam filters will filter those.

The average executive could potentially get hundreds of emails a day. When they get your email, they have to make an immediate decision to either open it, delete it, or save it. As a result, your email needs to be compelling enough for the recipient to open it and read it.

What to do? Avoid the things that will lower the probability of your email being delivered, opened, or read.

# TIP 73

## Personalization will get your email opened.

Having been in sales for a long time, the old spray and pray technique in prospecting is out, and personalization and customization is in. Here is what I have discovered over time. Prospects are more prone to ignore cookie cutter emails. Emails with subject lines that are not customized oftentimes are filtered or blocked. Because it is so easy to get on LinkedIn or a company website to conduct research before you contact a prospect, personalizing emails is easy.

In addition, when prospects notice that you have taken some time to do your research and customize and personalize your email, your credibility increases, and the probability of them opening and reading your email also increases.

Here are some ways to personalize your emails.

- **Use the prospect's name.** As we mentioned earlier in the book, a person's name is to that person the sweetest, most important sound in any language. Using the prospect's name in the subject line will increase the probability they will open the email.
- **Use what you know about them.** When I email prospects, I have a pretty good idea of who they work for, what they do, and what their pain points may be. So, I personalize my messaging around those factors, which helps me to grab their attention.
- **Mention trigger events.** While doing your research, it's possible that you were able to uncover a trigger event. Knowing trigger events helps you send an email that is very timely and relevant to the prospect.
- **Give a compliment.** My sales manager told me early on in my career that salespeople pay compliments because compliments

pay salespeople. Most people enjoy getting a compliment, particularly if it is genuine and sincere because it makes them feel good about themselves. Here are some things I compliment prospects on in and email:

- o   Recognition they have received in the industry or field.
- o   A post, video, or article they put on LinkedIn.
- o   The level of respect they have earned in their industry.

- **Mention their interests.** I get on LinkedIn and review my prospects' profiles and try to uncover the interests they have that I can use in the fabric of an email to gain their attention.
- **Reference a mutual connection.** I typically use the name of a mutual connection either in the subject line or in the first line of the body of the email.
- **Mention a pain point.** I try to personalize my emails based on a potential pain point the prospect may have. I may have learned about that pain point from my knowledge of current events in the industry or in speaking with someone who made me aware of the pain point. I personalize the pain point in three ways:

1.   The subject line.
2.   In the body of the email.
3.   In a concise case study on how I helped my clients that are similar to the prospect solve for that pain point.

What to do? Take the time, do the research, and find a point of connectivity to personalize your emails to increase the probability that your prospects will open, read, and respond to your email.

# TIP 74

# Use a personalized subject line.

The single biggest determinant of your email being opened is the subject line. You want to avoid some of the most common mistakes many people make, which are:

- Long subject lines. Shorter is better because it can be read quickly. Four to five words is ideal.
- Question marks. The first thing I do when I see a question mark in the subject line is delete it.
- Generic subject lines. These are not personalized or customized.

Based on what you know about the prospect from your research, you can customize and personalize your subject line. **The best subject lines:**

- **Use their name.**
  - o (Name), …

- **Use the name of a referral.**
  - o (Name) personal introduction.

- **Create urgency.**
  - o Season starts next month.

- **Touch on a pain point.**
  - o Helped (company) increase retention rate.

- **Reference a mutual connection.**
  - o (Name) spoke highly of you.

- **Compliment the prospect.**
  o   Congratulations on …

What to do? When personalizing the subject line of your emails, be creative. All you're trying to do is spark their interest, so they open your email.

# TIP 75

# Use an introductory prospecting email template.

A starting point for a good prospecting email is to have a framework or template you can follow for the majority of your emails. Having an introductory prospecting template you can customize and personalize will save you time. I have found that the introductory email is the most important email I send to new prospects. The email template I use consists of:

1. **Subject line**. Get their attention with a personalized subject line.
2. **Connect.** Have a compelling, personalized opening statement that helps create a connection between you and the prospect. This can be customized based on something you know about the prospect.
3. **Message.** Your message is typically your value proposition, ideally customized to the prospect. Your message can also be supported with case studies, names of clients you work with who are similar to the prospect, or how those clients benefit from working with you. The message should talk in terms of the prospect's interests and answer the question in the prospect's mind of WIIFM (what's in it for me?)
4. **Call to action.** You will want to end your email with a request – the call to action will typically be based on the reason you are sending the email in the first place. Hopefully, this will give you the result you are hoping to achieve.

   a. A meeting, virtual or in-person.
   b. Information to determine if they are a good fit.
   c. An introduction to a key stakeholder.

d.    Forward to other decision makers.

e.    What additional information can we provide you?

Example:

> **Subject Line:** Winning the War for Talent
>
> **Connect:** Hello, Keith, I just read an article on Advisor Hub from your CEO about how your company is focusing on recruiting this year which prompted me to reach out.
>
> **Message.** The reason for the email is that we have worked with a number of financial services firms, including Companies A, B, and C, helping them to train and coach their managers to become better recruiters.
>
> **Call to action.** How do you look either next Thursday or Friday to discuss what are you looking to accomplish with your recruiting efforts this year?

Once you have created the customized email, take a minute to review it for typos, errors, etc. before you hit send. The introductory email gives your prospect their first impression of you. Their first impression of you will be a good one if your email is good; it will be poor if your email is poorly written or unprofessional.

What to do? When sending introductory prospecting emails, use an introductory prospecting email template to work off of that you can personalize to your prospects. This will help you save time and improve the probability of the email being opened, read, and responded to.

# TIP 76

# Text when communicating with prospects.

A s you may know by now, I'm a big believer in using multiple modalities of communication when engaging with prospects. Texting is one of those modalities. I typically text prospects, because in certain situations it's the easiest and fastest way to communicate.

Here are the typical times when I text prospects.

- **Before a meeting,** I will send a text to my prospect to confirm the meeting time, location, and when I'm on my way. Since I go to a lot of office buildings with security, I also text my prospect when I arrive, so they know I'm in the building.
- **After I have a meeting,** I typically send a follow-up message, thanking them for the time we spent together, and if relevant I mention that I will send a summary of the meeting as a follow-up email.
- I check my **notifications on LinkedIn** every day to see who is having a birthday that day. Depending on who it is, I either send them a happy birthday message via LinkedIn or send them a happy birthday text.
- **After attending a networking event** if I have had a meaningful conversation with a prospect and exchange contact information, I will text them after the event. I tell them it was great to meet them and that I enjoyed the conversation. I also send them a connection request on LinkedIn at the same time and ask them if they would like to schedule a meeting and continue the conversation.

- **When I have not received a response** after making a recommendation, leaving voicemail messages, or sending emails, I send them a text. It's a last-ditch effort.

I have found that texting moves my prospects through my pipeline quicker.

**Texting dos and don'ts:**

- Try to **keep it business oriented.** If I have a personal relationship with the prospect, I send a more personal text. For example, the son of one of my prospects plays college basketball. When his son wins a game, I send him a personal text congratulating him on the win.
- **Keep it short and sweet.** When I send a text, I try to get right to the point, realizing that my prospects are really busy people. If I want to send something a little longer, I just send an email.
- **Send texts during business hours**. I work with prospects in different time zones. I try to be mindful of the time zone they are in and send during business hours for them, so it doesn't go through at the crack of dawn or at midnight.
- **Respond to texts in a timely manner.** I have two adult children, a twenty-three-year-old and a twenty-one-year-old, and I know they are all over their texts. If I don't get a response from them within five minutes of texting them, I know something is going on. When I get a text from a prospect, I want to be as responsive as possible.
- **Don't cold text.** I don't cold text because I don't like to be cold prospected via texting. As a result, I don't cold prospect via texting.

What to do? Use multiple modalities of communication when engaging with prospects. Include texting as one of the modalities when appropriate.

# CHAPTER 10

# FOLLOWING UP

# TIP 77

# Avoid these three questions on a follow-up call to gain a meeting.

I f I had a dollar for every darn foolish thing I have done in sales, I would be floating on a raft right now in the Caribbean drinking a Bahama Mama. I have made a ton of mistakes, let me tell you. One of them was in how I made follow-up calls to prospects. Countess times I have had meaningful initial conversations with prospects but for whatever reason was unable to set a meeting. Even though they did not give me a meeting, often times they would ask me to send them some information and give them a follow-up call. On these follow up calls, I finally learned the hard way what not to do.

I was asking a set of questions that I thought were the right questions to ask, but they weren't. From the school of hard knocks, here is what I learned not to do. Try to avoid asking the prospect as your first question, *"Did you get it?"* What I found when I asked that question is that, if they said *"No, I didn't get it,"* they would typically say, "Could you resend it and follow up with me again?" Or they would say, *"Could you resend it, and I will get back to you?"* In either case, I was lengthening the sales cycle or losing control of the process.

The second question I would ask them, if they said they got it was *"Did you read it?"* What I discovered by asking them that question was that they had to admit to me that they didn't read it when the reality of it was that they were never going to read it because their request was actually their put-off objection. I was making them feel bad about not doing something they were never going to do anyway. That being said, there is a subset of prospects who will actually read the information. I still avoid that question anyway.

To compound my buffoonery, if I got that far with the third question, I would then ask them if they did get it and read it was, *"Do you have any questions?"* What do you think their answer was 99% of the time? Of course, it was no. Where to go from there? It's hard to rebound from a no.

I learned to avoid asking these three questions after I sent any information:

- Did you get it?
- Did you read it?
- Do you have any questions?

What I began to do instead is this three-step process on my follow-up calls.

**Step one:** I reintroduce myself.

**Step two:** I bring the prospect back to prior conversations by reviewing what we discussed.

**Step three:** I present my offer of value and recommend getting together for a meeting.

It goes something like this.

> Good morning, (name), this is Steve Johnson with the Next Level. How have you been?
>
> (Name), from our past conversation, your company's major priority this year is to bring in new accounts. Is that right? You also mentioned that you were open to partnering with someone from the outside to help you with this. Is that still true? You mentioned that you were going to put this out to bid soon. Is that accurate?
>
> (Name), let's **get together** for a cup of coffee. I can learn more about you and let you know how we work with our clients. We may be able to **add value** to your situation because we work with companies just like yours, helping them to bring in new accounts. If there is a **good fit**, we can discuss possible next steps. How do you look next week?

The difference between what <u>not to do</u> and what <u>to do</u> is really simple. In what <u>to do</u>, you will use the notes you took from the prior conversation, and as you summarize those notes your goal is to get the prospect to say yes, yes, and yes. You want the physiology and anatomy of their entire being to be in the yes, yes, yes mode before you ask them to get together for a meeting. It doesn't mean that they won't say no, but after they have said yes three times in a row the probability that they will say yes when you ask them for a meeting goes up. This is the "I like it, I love it, I want some more of it" close for a meeting.

What to do? On your follow up calls, if you have sent the prospect any information at all, try to avoid these three questions:

- Did you get it?
- Did you read it?
- Do you have any questions?

Instead go for the "I like it, I love it, I want some more of it" close by getting the prospect to say the word every salesperson loves to hear three times in a row, the word "yes." Woo!

# TIP 78

# Stay top of mind with prospects in your pipeline.

Generally speaking, prospects work on their own timeline. There are times that their timeline is in synch with yours, and there are times when it is not. You could think that your timeline is in synch, but their timeline can change. Sometimes it speeds up, which is great, and sometimes it slows down. Nevertheless, it always makes sense to stay top of mind with prospects wherever they are in the pipeline.

So here are five tips to stay top-of-mind with prospects in your pipeline.

Tip number one is to **be active on social media**. I have an eight-step daily LinkedIn routine that I created so that I could be consistent with my activity on social media. The routine has real metrics attached to it, such as likes, comments, or shares per day, posts per week, and comments on any notifications. What I have found is that this type of activity enables me to be relevant with thought leadership and timely with my comments to keep my brand top of mind.

Tip number two is to **update your website**. This will give you opportunities for greater exposure to your prospects. Most of the opportunities in my pipeline are with multiple decision makers. You never know who is going to go to your website at the point when they are thinking about making a decision. You want it to make a positive impression. We just updated ours with our best-selling books, case studies, offerings, and written and video blogs. We want to be better positioned for success by showcasing our capabilities on our website.

Tip number three is to **demonstrate your skills on video**. This is hands down one of the fastest growing methods to reach out to and stay top of mind with prospects. I have made over one hundred videos and post them on LinkedIn, our website, and our YouTube channel. Nothing too fancy. People buy from people. Video gives them a chance to see the real you. If you have a prospect in your pipeline, I think if they see you on video, they will be more likely to move to the next step with you.

Tip number four is to follow up. There could be opportunities in your pipeline that don't follow your typical sales cycle and timeline. Moving certain prospects to clients requires a lot of follow-up calls, emails, voicemails, additional information, and other follow-up activities. What I have discovered is that a timely follow-up helps you build your credibility with prospects and goes a long way in improving your chances of success.

Tip number five is to send a gift. You don't want to be over the top here. I have found one gift that works better than any other gift I have tried to send to prospects or clients in my pipeline. It's See's Candy. You can send it at any time. A box of nuts and chews is less than $25, and whoever you send it to is a hero. They enjoy it themselves or share it with their co-workers or their family. You will be top of mind in a positive way.

The bottom line is that staying top of mind requires creativity and a positive mindset. What to do? Identify one opportunity in your pipeline and determine what you can do to stay top of mind.

# TIP 79

# A yes or a no is better than a maybe. Four strategies for a stalled sale.

So, let's assume you have taken a prospect through your sales process, which has lasted the length your normal sales cycle, and they still haven't moved forward. What do you do? If you feel so inclined, you may want to try to move the prospect to a decision. The benefit to you is saving everyone's time, especially your own. If you receive a "no" from the prospect, it does not mean that you have to write them off forever. It just means they are not ready to move forward right now. You can always follow up with them at any time. You can then use the time you were spending on that prospect to put more prospects in the top of your pipeline.

So, here are four strategies you may want to consider for a stalled sale. If you like any of them, use what works for you, and don't get hung up on the ones that won't work for you.

The first strategy is to **uncover the obstacle that is blocking their way forward**. Simply ask the prospect why they are not moving forward with your recommendation.

> (Prospect's name), we've had a number of meetings. We had an initial get-to-know-you meeting over the phone, after that we had a second meeting with your sales leadership team, and then we conducted a focus group with your sales staff. From that, we were able to present you with a proposal. We believe we could add value based on our understanding of your situation as well as our experience in working with other financial services firms that are similar to you. (Prospect's name), just out of curiosity, what's preventing you from moving forward?

The second strategy is to **ask the prospect for their advice** on how they would like to see you follow up with them moving forward. If you never want to ask a prospect to make a decision because you feel like you are being pushy or salesy, you never have to. Just ask them for their advice, and they will tell you what to do.

> (Prospect's name), we've had a number of meetings. We had an initial get to know you meeting over the phone, after that we had a second meeting with your sales leadership team, and then we conducted a focus group with your sales staff. From that, we were able to present you with a proposal. We believe we could add value based on our understanding of your situation as well as our experience in working with other financial services firms that are similar to you. (Prospect's name), what advice would you give me on how to follow up with you moving forward?

The third strategy is to **proactively bring up the concern that you think may be causing them to hesitate.** In all of your interactions with the prospect, they may have given you a cue or a clue as to what is holding them back. Sometimes when proactively bringing up the concern you think the prospect may have, your instincts are correct, and you can address the concern. Other times though, bringing up the concern you think is blocking them from moving forward, you uncover their real concern. This is your ideal scenario.

> (Prospect's name), we've had a number of meetings. We had an initial get-to-know-you meeting over the phone, after that we had a second meeting with your sales leadership team, and then we conducted a focus group with your sales staff. From that, we were able to present you with a proposal. We believe we could add value based on our understanding of your situation as well as our experience in working with other financial services firms that are similar to you. (Prospect's name), I sense that you are concerned about our fee structure. Is that right? Let's talk about that.

The fourth strategy is to **simply ask the prospect for a yes or a no.** There are instances when a prospect will drag the sales cycle on and on. They are indecisive and may never be happy with what they are offered. In the end, you need to determine are they a suspect or a prospect.

(Prospect's name), we've had a number of meetings. We had an initial get-to-know-you meeting over the phone, after that we had a second meeting with your sales leadership team, and then we conducted a focus group with your sales staff. From that, we were able to present you with a proposal. We believe we could add value based on our understanding of your situation as well as our experience in working with other financial services firms that are similar to you. (Prospect's name), I have to ask, are you curious or are you serious? If implementing this sales training is not a priority at this time, no problem. We can revisit it at another time. But, if it is a priority, how about we talk about the next steps?

Moving a prospect to a decision is one of the most liberating things you can do in sales. You can finally try to determine why a prospect is not moving forward to the next step with you. They can stop ghosting you, and you can move on the next prospect. Having had thousands of these conversations with prospects in over thirty-six years of sales, one thing I have observed is that when a prospect feels like you are willing to walk away, they often let down their guard and are forthcoming with the real reason they are not moving forward with you. The benefit to you is if you are able to address the real concern you may be able to move to the next step. If not, spend your time putting more prospects in the top of the pipeline.

What to do? Identify one stalled sale and try to move the prospect to a decision using one of these strategies.

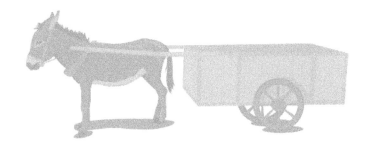

# CHAPTER 11

# OVERCOMING OBJECTIONS TO A MEETING

# TIP 80

# Objections are coming. Shame on you if you're not ready.

I n my first two weeks in sales, my manager told me to write down every objection that I got from prospects who blocked me from getting meetings. It did not take too long to see that I was getting the same five objections about 90 to 95% of the time. The bulk of the time, I heard I'm too busy, I'm not interested, the program costs too much, the night of the week you are offering the class doesn't work, and the location isn't convenient for me.

So, Los Angeles just hosted the Olympics in 1984, and my sales manager asked me if I knew the name of our gold medal hurdler.

I said, "Of course I do. It's Edwin Moses."

He said, "When Edwin Moses runs the hurdles, does he know the hurdles are there?"

I said, "Yes, he does."

He said, "That's right. He knows the hurdles are there, but he prepares, practices, and trains to run the hurdles better than anyone in the world. He is the best. You told me after two weeks of making calls you got the same five objections about 90-95% of the time. Is that right?"

I said, "Yes."

He said, just like Edwin Moses prepares, practices, and trains to run the hurdles, you need to **prepare, practice, and train** to handle those five objections, because you know they are coming, just like Edwin Moses knows the race has hurdles. Shame on you if you're not ready.

So, let's get you ready to handle objections because you know they're coming.

# TIP 81

# Three step process to handling objections to a meeting.

N o matter how we deliver sales training, whether digitally, virtually, or in person, the topic most of our clients want and enjoy the most is a good old-fashioned objection handling clinic. Why is that? Because, if you have made a lot of calls, you realize that you are an interruption in the prospect's day. You probably don't like to be interrupted, and neither do they. From my experience, there are three different ways a prospect reacts to the interruption.

1. Yes, I'm interested.
2. No, I'm not interested.
3. Maybe.

If it is a yes, go for a meeting. If it is a hard no, move on. Not all no's are created equal. Where further developing your skill at handling objections will make a difference is in the maybe.

The first thing you want to do to get ready to **turn maybes into meetings** is to have a process. The three-step process I recommend is to acknowledge the objection, respond to the objection, and then ask the prospect again to get together for a meeting.

- Step one is to **acknowledge the objection with a cushion phrase** to soften the blow. For example:
  o   I get it.
  o   I hear you.
- Step two is to **respond to the objection**. There are multiple ways you can do this.
  o   You can ask questions, then respond.
  o   You can respond and then ask questions.

o   You can just respond.

- Step three is to **ask the prospect for a meeting**. Often this step is forgotten or left out after responding. At the end of the day, you gotta ask the prospect to meet.

Here is an example that demonstrates all three steps of the process.

**Step one: Acknowledge and Cushion:** (Name), I thought that you would be working with a competitor.

**Step two: Respond**: That is the reason we should get together. Our meeting will do one of two things. Through comparison, you will be able to determine if your current provider is truly meeting your needs, or you might find out that there are other options available to you. You win both ways.

**Step three: Ask for the meeting.** How about we get together on either Monday or Tuesday for coffee?

This is the reversal method. The very reason why they say they don't want to meet is the exact reason they should. It is an unconventional response that is different than what they typically hear, which improves your odds of getting a meeting. There is an inherent benefit to them in meeting with you. They will either gain affirmation that their current provider is doing a great job, or they may discover there is room for improvement.

When trying to get meetings, you're going to get objections. As a result, you want to have a process you can follow that gives you confidence.

What to do? Think about the three-step process and how you can customize your responses using this process. Use it when a prospect gives you an objection to a meeting.

# TIP 82

# How to handle "I'm all set."

**"I**'m all set." We have all heard it before. It is possible that some prospects are not as "all set" as they think they are. So here are three examples of how to handle this objection and set a meeting.

1. That's great, (name)! We appreciate loyalty from our clients as well. There may be opportunities that we can provide that are not available through your current vendor. Why don't we get together for a cup of coffee to explore some possibilities?

   - One positive element of this response is that it is conceivable that **you have capabilities** that are not available to the prospect through who they are currently working with.

2. I hear what you're saying (name). It is possible that what we do might compliment what you are already doing. It is not uncommon for organizations like yours to work with multiple vendors. It never hurts to see what else is out there. Would you be available next Tuesday or Wednesday for a cup of coffee?

   - One positive element of this response is you're **not asking them to make a change.** You are just asking them to get together.

3. (Name,) I understand. I'd be surprised if you told me otherwise. Many of our customers had other vendors when we first met. It could be worthwhile for you to meet with us, because we can give you a second opinion or competitive bid that could help you determine if you are getting the best value from your current provider. How do you look next week?

- One positive element of this response is you **are offering to give them a second opinion** or competitive bid to help them confirm they are getting the best value for their money.

The key to these responses is that you are not trying to tell them that they are <u>not</u> all set. With your response, you are trying to pique their interest enough to see if they are open to getting together.

What to do? Determine which of these responses would work best for you, then customize them to fit what you do and your personality. Write it down, practice it over, over, and over again. Use it when you hear someone say, "I'm all set."

# TIP 83

# How to handle "I'm not interested."

**"I**'m not interested" could be a knee-jerk reaction—a brush-off response. As a result, you want to have some standard responses ready that ideally get the prospect interested.

1. (Name), thanks for letting me know that up front. We work with other business owners helping them with their IT needs so they can spend their time growing their business. I don't know if we can add any value, but maybe we can. How about coffee next week?

    - The benefit of this response is that you quickly get your **value proposition** out to pique their interest by communicating that you work with others similar to them. If they are still not interested, you have at least planted the seed that you are experienced in working with people like them.

2. (Name), I can understand that. Quick question. Do you know exactly how much money it's going to take for you to retire when you plan to—and to stay retired? Why don't we get together at no cost or obligation to you to help you figure it out? How does next Wednesday after work sound?

    - One of the most searched financial topics on the internet is, "How much do I need to retire?" This response **plays into the question that may be going on in many investors' minds.**

3. No problem, (name). Quick question. What would have to change in your situation to make you more open to a conversation like this in the future?

- The power of this response is it **shifts the prospect's mind-set** from their brush-off response to potentially thinking about why they should have a conversation with you.

4. (Name), I understand how you **feel**. In fact, many of our clients who are corporate executives, like you, **felt** the same way when we first contacted them. They went ahead and had a brief meeting with us, and what they **found** was that we could add value to their situation because of our experience in working with corporate executives. Would sometime in the morning or afternoon be better?

- This response is called **"feel, felt, found."** This is the oldest objection handling technique of all time. Why? Because it **works**.

What to do? Determine which of these responses would work best for you, then customize them to fit what you do and your personality. Write it down, practice it over, over, and over again. Use it when you hear someone say, "I'm not interested."

# TIP 84

# How to handle "I'm too busy."

As with any put off or stall, this objection is easy to handle if you take the time to learn a few responses and use them with confidence. So here are three examples.

1. (Name), I can certainly understand that! I thought you would be. Most successful corporate executives are very busy. Because of this, they find the easiest time to get together is before work. How about we have coffee next week?

    - There are several things I like about this response. Number one, it's **unconventional**. When the prospect says they're busy, I agree with them and compliment them. Secondarily, I've discovered that when a prospect agrees to meet for breakfast, they are more **qualified**, they get to their problem **quickly**, there are **less cancellations**, and if it matters it's the **least expensive** meal of the day.

2. (Name), I understand that you're busy. But everyone has to eat! How about we have lunch together next week? I can come to you.

    - This response may be hokey, but it's also **unconventional**. Prospects are used to cold callers and their typical responses. Anything you say that is out of the normal pattern **disrupts their thought process** and improves the odds of you setting a meeting.

3.  (Name), I get it. Quick question. Is recruiting a priority for your firm this year?

    •   You want to **acknowledge** they are busy then **ask a quick question** to determine if they have a need or pain point that could lead to further conversation.

What to do? Determine which of these responses would work best for you then customize it to fit what you do and your personality. Write it down, practice it over, over, and over again. Use it when you hear someone say, "I'm too busy."

# TIP 85

# How to handle
# "Email me some information."

can't tell you how many times a prospect has said to me "send me some information." This potential stall has evolved over time. It started with send me..., then went to fax me..., now it is email me... It still means the same thing. They don't want to take the time to talk with you when you call, or they don't have a perceived need.

If you just send them something, it sets up the chase after the send, which is, "Did you get it?" "Did you read it?" "Do you have any questions?"

The way to try to **avoid the chase** is to ask questions upfront to determine if they are a prospect or a suspect before you send them anything and waste each other's time.

1. (Name), I would be happy to do that. What's your email address? While I have you on the phone, let me ask you two questions to determine whether or not it even makes sense for me to follow up with you.

   What information would you like to see? If you like what you see, what do you think would be the next step for us?

   • This approach is good because you get their email address. You get the specific type of information they want to see. If the information fits their criteria, it lets you know if they are interested in taking the next step.

2. (Name), I have enough information to fill up the Library of Congress, but I don't want to blow up your inbox. Let me ask you a few quick questions so that I can send you information that is specific to you.

What is your email? What information would you like to see? If you like what you see, what do you think would be the next step for us?

- This approach is like the previous example but is a little more humorous. It's a little more unconventional. Because it's different, it might create an environment that is more informal and engaging.

What to do? Determine which of these responses would work best for you, then customize it to fit what you do and your personality. Write it down, practice it over, over, and over again. Use it when you hear someone say, "Email me some information."

# TIP 86

# How to handle
# "No need right now."

**W**hether or not a prospect has a need when you give them a call, you still want to meet with them anyway so that when they do have a need you are top of mind. **One constant in life is change.** When a change in their life occurs that causes the need for what you do, you will be well be in a better position to earn their business.

1.  (Name), you might not have a need right now, but in my experience, I have found that people are most successful when they begin thinking about and planning for a potential need in advance. How do you look next week for coffee?

    •   This response is a good one because you are **planting a seed** with them on the importance of planning and being prepared. Before our kids applied to colleges, we visited the schools they wanted to get in to. So, when they got their acceptance letters, we were in a more informed position to make a decision.

2.  No worries, (name). Things have a way of changing over time. Because of that, would you have any objection if I kept in touch with you every three months? In the meantime, if you are comfortable giving me your email address, I can send you a one-pager on our capabilities so you're more familiar with what we do.

    •   This response **leaves the door open** for a future follow-up. When they agree with you, they will be more open to having a conversation in the future. You also have an opportunity to send them an introductory email, so they know a little more about you and what you do. Sometimes the information can pique their interest.

What to do? Determine which of these responses would work best for you, then customize them to fit what you do and your personality. Write it down, practice it over, over, and over again. Use it when you hear, "No need right now."

# TIP 87

# How to handle
# "I'm working with a competitor."

One of the most common objections you will probably get when trying to set a meeting is, "I'm working with a competitor."

1.  That's good, (name). If you're open to it, we can give you a second set of eyes on your situation. We may be able to add some value. If you think we can, it's up to you if you want to move forward. How do you look next week for lunch?

    - A couple positive elements of this response. It **offers value** with a second set of eyes and **leaves it up to them** to take the next step.

2.  (Name), the number one reason new clients come to us is for better service. What type of service are you getting from your current vendor? If you're open to it, I can show you what we do differently, and then you can decide for yourself if you would like to take the next step. How about getting together on Thursday or Friday afternoon for coffee?

    - In working with over 90,000 salespeople, a big reason they say they get meetings is because their prospect is currently receiving **poor service**. This response plays into that scenario.

3.  That's great (name), how long have you been working with them?

    Has it been that long since you have compared their service with someone else's? A lot has changed in that time. It sounds like now would be a good time for you to see what else is out there. How open are you to meeting with us at no cost or obligation to you?

- Many prospects are proud of the long-lasting relationship they have had with their vendors, but in a **dynamic and changing environment** it is possible that it could be in their best interest to see what else is out there.

4. Awesome, (name). If you are truly happy with them, you shouldn't even think about making a change. I just wanted to see if you were interested in meeting for fifteen minutes to see if we are a good fit. The benefit to you is that, if you needed to make a change in the future, you would at least know your options. What day next week works best for you for coffee?

- The strength of this response is that you are **not asking them to make a change**. You are just offering to get together with them to let them know what their options would be if they needed to make a change in the future.

5. That's great, (name). How long have you been working with them?

How did you decide to work with them?

What do you wish they did better?

How open would you be to meeting with us to compare services?

How do you look next week for coffee?

- The strength of this response is that you are **trying to uncover a pain point**. Maybe they haven't been working with them that long, maybe it was an inherited account, maybe they are not getting the service they want, or they may be open-minded to seeing what else is out there.

It is possible that some prospects are not as happy with their current vendor as they think they are. The key to these responses is that you are not trying to tell them that they should leave their current vendor. You are just seeing if they are open-minded enough to get together.

What to do? Determine which of these responses would work best for you, then customize it to fit what you do and your personality. Write it down, practice it over, over, and over again. Use it when you hear someone say, "I'm working with a competitor."

# TIP 88

# Four ways to get better at handling objections to a meeting.

Here are four ways to get better at handling objections to help you turn more maybes into meetings.

1. **Don't take rejection personally.**

   Over time, I realized that not every prospect wanted or needed what I sold. What I focused on were the ones who did. Rejection is part of the game. Accept it and put it in its proper perspective. Expect rejection and don't take it personally. Just move on.

2. **Script out your responses.**

   Take the time to carefully script out responses to the most common objections you get day in and day out. Remember the best thing about prospecting is that you know you will get the same concerns, questions, stalls, and put-offs over and over again.

3. **Practice your responses.**

   Practice your responses until they become second nature. By internalizing your responses through repetitive practice, you will be able to handle objections without even thinking about them.

4. **Put your responses where you can see them when prospecting.**

   Take a three-by-five card and put your responses in a place where you can see them when prospecting. This will help to build your confidence. The more prepared you are for the no, the more confident you will be in asking for the yes.

What to do? Before making calls, script out responses to the most common objections you hear when asking for a meeting. Practice them and put them there where you can see them when you are prospecting. If your prospect still turns you down, don't take it personally. Just move on.

I'm going to close this book just as I started it. I have made more mistakes and lost more sales in the last thirty-eight years than just about anybody I know. The opportunities lost from all those mistakes cost me a lot. But in this laboratory of human experience, this gauntlet I have run has enabled me over time to learn what works and doesn't work. I was able to learn some best practices from high-performing salespeople along the way. Prospecting can be one of the most difficult parts of the sales process. Hopefully you found at least one or two nuggets of useful information that will help you in your prospecting efforts.

My intention for writing this book was to share with you the experience and knowledge I gained prospecting as I walked the walk and talked the talk.

Now, are you ready to get out there and make some sales? Get fired up, and make it happen!